Edutocracy:
My Time Behind Public Education's
Iron Curtain

Edutocracy:
My Time Behind Public Education's Iron Curtain

Dr. Brian M. Erskine

Verum Publishing
2013

Edutocracy: My Time Behind Public Education's Iron Curtain

Copyright © 2013 by Brian M. Erskine

First Printing: 2013

ISBN 978-0-9910365-0-9 (Paperback)
ISBN 978-0-9910365-1-6 (Hardcover)
ISBN 978-0-9910365-2-3 (ebook)

Also available as an eBook for Kindle and Nook
at www.vook.com and at iBookstore

Verum Publishing
Virginia

Ordering Information:

Special discounts are available on quantity purchases by corporations, associations, educators, and others. For details, contact the publisher at the phone number below.

U.S. trade bookstores and wholesalers:
Please contact Verum Publishing
Tel: (540) 735-0818; or email verumpublishing@nym.hush.com

Dedication

*To my beautiful wife, Sarah, without whom
I wouldn't be able to be.*

*To the people who chose to turn their backs
when the going got tough, I forgive you.*

Preface

If you've ever tried to keep weeds from growing in your garden then you'll understand this metaphor. Educrats seek to clear the ground of everyone and everything they see as debris. They've placed their weed fabric on the ground, covered it with decorative stones, and enclosed the whole garden in brick borders. This book is about the small pesky rock under the fabric that wears a hole over time. It's a salute to the bird flying overhead that makes a deposit of seeds in the rocks and the dog that digs through the flowers and exposes the soil to the sunlight.

Introduction

Here are a few important editorial notes and points of guidance for readers. This book is an account of my life and experiences. Although every iota of narrative detail is unfiltered, I chose to change all of the identifying information pertaining to these stories. With the exception of one identified and positive name-drop in the first chapter, I changed the names, gender, and identifying attributes of the subjects in order to ensure the book remains about the stories and not any particular person. Additionally, I chose not to identify the names of any institutions or agents thereof.

You will see several politically-charged statements throughout this book, some of which will upset my fellow Conservatives and sensible Libertarians while most will outrage the Liberal audience. I'm an equal opportunity rabble-rouser. What I can say, definitively, is that my pedigree is political and that despite my best attempts at concealing it, that persona shines through the rest. Most importantly, this story is not political.

My purpose for writing this book is strictly catharsis. Despite my extensive writing for private publications and contributions to textbooks in the past, this is the first public release bearing my name. Like teaching, there is no fortune to be made writing books. One does so because they have a message to send and a story to tell. This is my story.

Chapter 1—Getting in the Door

It's no big secret that landing a teaching gig in this unending and deepening recession is tough. The teacher preparation programs recruit young people who sincerely want to teach and mentor children as well as those college-age people seeking to relive the glory of their high school years. They tell you that there are teacher shortages and critical needs areas that are just waiting to be filled upon graduation. They fail to mention that these vacant positions are often in inner city schools with metal detectors, students who are, or are soon to be criminals, and hostile communities.

Alternative paths to teaching are even allowing public and private institutions to recruit older workers and non-education professionals into so-called "career changer" programs. These programs retrain degreed professionals to use their subject area degrees and add supplemental teaching certification. I know because I went through one of these programs to become a public school teacher.

Constantly concerned over their placement rates, these programs seek to advertise that their graduates are among the fastest placed teachers in the country. To that end, entire classes are dedicated to landing a faculty job. Not to be confused with "How to interview" workshops, these classes create interviewee machines. From what to say and how to smile to the type of blouses and ties to choose, these programs stake their reputation on graduates becoming success stories and agreeing to appear in promotional materials with a broad smile in front of a classroom of children.

When I decided to make the jump to teaching secondary education I did so because I was disillusioned with the impersonal nature of teaching in higher education and unfulfilled by working to make a stranger wealthy. Don't get me wrong though; I am a capitalist from top to bottom. History proves and I agree that employment as a worker bee is great for the bee, the hive, and the surrounding fields. My problem is that I'm not a corporate guy. I don't work well in a hierarchy unless I'm either at the top of it or an independent contractor.

I had already earned a graduate degree and completed some of my doctoral work when I lost interest in the crumbling ivory tower. Working for a not for profit as well as working as a government contractor gave me a front row seat to observe some of the most lavish and nauseating spending of tax dollars. After Federally-funded junkets to cities around the U.S. that accomplished essentially nothing, I simply couldn't stomach the waste anymore and ended up reporting the entity for misuse of Federal grant dollars that they were later forced to repay. I was officially stuck trying to decide what I wanted to do with years of education and job experience at a very young age.

I was instantly drawn in by the prospect of a career that would allow me to go home every day knowing I did something meaningful and enriching for myself and someone else. I'd been terrified of reaching retirement and looking back over my career only to see spreadsheets, archived email, and feel as if I had wasted my time. Teaching young people about the subject I care about and having the chance to be a role model for some of them seemed like the perfect move. I knew that I was an academic first, but the library in my head was worthless if I didn't share it.

I knew going in that anyone in the teaching profession looking for good money was in the wrong business. In fact, my first teaching job boasted a lower annual salary than that of the 19 year old high school dropout who picked up my garbage at the curb once per week. I had taken the altruistic position that I was doing something intangibly rewarding that paid enough of a salary to live an honest working lifestyle. Luckily, my wife had an outstanding job with great benefits that allowed me to settle for a pittance at my career.

Once I had talked myself into teaching at the secondary level it was time to start checking boxes. I was blessed to find a great transition program that placed me in a cohort of about 12 other people. We spent 6 months working full time while attending marathon length classes and weekend sessions. Although I had a great deal of teaching experience and had already earned the credentials to teach in higher education, the administrative hoops of k-12 required a lot more time. Not only did I have to take out a private loan to pay for the money-grubbing program, but I also spent hundreds in standardized licensing tests and certifications. Remember, unlike doctors who can justify their expensive training, teachers have to spend exorbitantly to live meagerly.

Among the topics covered by the program there were two that I actually enjoyed: classroom management, and dealing with parents. In higher ed. I had been able, and required, to ignore helicopter parents due to privacy laws and the adult age of the students. This new career brought with it no such luck. I was a total newbie when it came to discipline and parental contact, and I am eternally thankful for the lessons I learned during that period of the program. The lady who taught the portion of the program regarding classroom management was actually the mother of a former schoolmate of mine. Dr. Fred Jone's "Tools for teaching" is a great read and a book that all teachers should read before deciding on a classroom management strategy. The other components of the program, however, were not as beneficial.

Much like breaking a horse for the first time, this program made no illusions about its intent to "rewire" us to think like "good teachers." From the forcible indoctrination of failed instructional practices like classroom differentiation (tiered classrooms) and performance-based grading to the scourge of multiple option assessment, we were molded into compliance with a particular failed educational ideology. Rightly or not, this rewiring was necessary, or so we were told, to be a marketable candidate for a teaching job. We were the people in the velvet rope line outside an exclusive club, and if we didn't either know the bouncer or the code word to whisper, we didn't stand a chance of getting in.

As part of the reconditioning process, our cohort underwent extensive training regarding the buzzwords we would need to know and discuss conversationally to satisfy the interviewer's checklist. Among those words and phrases were "disadvantaged students," "low socio-economic background," and "underserved populations." We were taught to give answers that were open-ended and essentially meaningless so as to allow the interviewer to hear whatever it is they wanted from the interviewee. On the other side of the interview table, the interviewer was equally culpable in the box checking game. They were also trained and conditioned to literally place checkmarks beside keywords and phrases that showed a candidate's familiarity with the district's preordained buzzwords and established the candidate as legitimate.

At one point the program's faculty advisor shared with us some of the questions we were likely to encounter when we went looking for a teaching position at a public school. The greatest hits included questions like these:

"How do you plan to teach differently to diverse students?" "How would you change your lessons to accommodate students who refuse to do their work?" "Who is at fault when a teacher gives the student all the support available, but the student still fails?"

Like good soldiers of the cause we were taught to speak in the language of victimology. We became proficient at rattling off lines like "regardless of gender, race, ethnicity, income status, citizenship status, and sexual orientation." These phrases were intended to show hiring principals that we were willing to comply with the expected norms and acceptable prevailing ideology of the system. Similarly, there was a list of off-limits words that were interview death knells. Failure, detention, slow, lazy, and student responsibility were all stricken from our vocabulary.

At one point in the latter stages of the program, I dared to start asking questions. Having already proudly and intentionally earned a reputation in my cohort as the independent, I inadvertently unearthed some of my peers' inner rabble rousing tendencies. Any time we challenged the reconditioning process and the implantation of scientifically unsupported or brazenly biased information we were swiftly rebuked for distracting other students. Despite how it may have appeared, we didn't have the benefit of hindsight at the time; we honestly had disagreement and confusion over what we were being taught because it just didn't feel right.

The preparation program was designed to be completed before participants actually became teachers. Fortunately, I stumbled upon an opening in a nearby school district for a high school U.S. Government teacher about half-way through the program. This break officially made me the first (and ultimately one of the few) to actually become a teacher. Even after I started teaching full time, I was still attending the reconditioning camp for several hours every week. At one point, the verbose narcissist who ran the program grew openly hostile to me for short circuiting his program's intended chronology and sharing my limited experiences with my cohort.

As the months and years went on, I stayed in semi-regular contact with many of the folks in the program. I befriended one man in particular whom I admired a great deal. With his permission, I'll quickly sing Don's praises because he is the rare type of man who would never do it himself. Don was an older man in his fifties who had retired from business and human resources looking for a second and more fulfilling career. What he lacked in technological savvy he more than made up with his knowledge of U.S. history and life experiences. In an already difficult job market for teachers, he faced increasingly difficult odds securing a teaching position because of implicit discrimination against his age and lack of classroom experience. To this day, I continue to admire Don's toughness during the class and his tenacity in maintaining values he knew to be solid in the face of the reconditioning program.

Chapter 2—Landing the Gig

I was working in the mold-ridden basement of a D.C. metro area government contractor as a professional proposal writer when I received an unexpected call. I had been applying for every teaching vacancy within 75 miles of my home for the past six months hoping to teach on a provisional license. This call came right about the time my health had seen its much better days and my descent into permanent "Office Space" employment was well on its way to becoming permanent. The social studies department chair from one of the schools to which I had only recently applied called to leave me a welcoming interview invitation with the sound of chatting students in the background.

With padfolio in hand and armed to the hilt with my talking points, I introduced myself to the student aid working at the secretary's desk. I was greeted warmly and asked to register on the elaborate security system as a guest and have my photo and information printed onto a disposable adhesive badge. As I waited there in the lobby of the office that would soon be my school, I had no idea what to expect.

The Virginia community where I was interviewing was unique in its character. It was a rural agricultural hub that had recently become a bedroom community for higher paid government workers and contractors in the greater Washington, D.C. metropolitan area. The population was split between the native farming families, the rich transplants, a growing illegal immigrant population, and a permanent underclass of minorities reliant upon taxpayer assistance to survive.

I was welcomed into the principal's office by a bear of a man with a smile on his face. Having already been phone interviewed by his assistant and the head of the social studies department, I was familiar with the basics of the position and the situation. This man who we'll call Tom was my first actual exposure to a very new place.

Tom had explained to me over the phone that the position was to start as a long-term substitute job for a teacher that was embroiled in a personnel matter and unlikely to return, upon which time the position would become permanent. You can imagine how cautious I was about leaving a nearly six figure career for a tentative shot at a position paying about 45 percent of my current salary. Despite my apprehension, I was enamored by Tom's words as he told me the story about how he had opened the new school only a few years before after serving as a designer and construction principal.

His philosophy of education was like a near photocopy of my own at the time. Having expected to deliver my pre-rehearsed lines, I was pleasantly surprised when he engaged me in a conversation about my teaching style and my thoughts on important education matters. With the physical and intellectual presence of a giant, Tom already had me hooked, and I think he knew it. After an extensive tour of the building and an equally informative description explaining why he had designed the school into grade level houses and a central teacher collaboration area, I was admittedly a little charmed.

Having already gotten the green light from my wife to accept the position, Tom dispatched one of the three other highly paid assistant principals to take over the tour.

The tour concluded, and I was sent to the school district's central administration building just a few miles away to begin the hiring paperwork process. What I saw there and the brief interactions I had there were a picture-perfect forecast for what was to come in the next three years.

As a physically handicapped person, I parked in the designated area nearly 50 feet away from a staircase entrance to a monolithic outdated building and multipurpose middle school. I immediately noticed the extravagant vehicles around me. These luxury class vehicles were a far cry from the consumer-grade commuter cars I had seen at the high school only moments ago.

When I entered the building I was immediately taken by the decrepit appearance of everything I saw. Stained and peeling walls and ceilings and 1960s era attributes made me rethink the luxury standards I had seen outside. Each supposedly important person in the building had a special placard outside their office suite denoting haughty titles like "Assistant Superintendent for …" and "Senior Director of …" Their secretaries played their dutiful roles eyeing me to see which suite I was headed for and smiled as I passed by.

I had no sooner reached the Human Resources Office when I noticed the place was empty. There were no "Out to lunch" signs or posted schedules. There was an empty receptionist's desk and an open conference room door. In there were a handful of folks idly chatting and eating around a table that took up the entire room and resembled the executive board room table from a Fortune 500 company. After several minutes of patiently waiting, the receptionist saw me and came to greet me, though the greeting was obviously only a cold formality.

She began to process my paperwork when a deep, abrasive, and country-twanged voice bellowed from the conference room saying something like "He can wait til later, we're busy." The receptionist paid him no mind and continued taking my photograph for my identification credentials. I sat there wondering what type of customer service I was about to receive from a clearly deficient office of taxpayer funded employees.

Having received such a warm welcome at the school, I decided to dismiss the gruffness and unprofessionalism of the man I'd encountered as a fluke and the upside down disparities I observed at the central office. With paperwork processed and identification badge affixed, I was officially a twelfth grade U.S. Government teacher.

Chapter 3—Walking into the Fire

No amount of preparation or instruction could have prepared me for what I was about to experience. As I walked into the school building and entered the inner office area, I was surrounded by teachers milling around in a hurried mess of papers, kicking photocopiers, and ranting about their least favorite student's most recent incident. Not wishing to get distracted from my well planned morning, I briskly made my way to my new classroom.

It was early enough in the morning that the students hadn't yet begun to arrive, and the hallways were still quiet except for the tapping of high heels of teachers as they practically ran down the hallways. I turned the key, opened the door, and just stared as I soaked in my new home. The previous teacher's belongings were still strewn throughout the room, as were his students' clothes, books, and garbage. Nonetheless, I went about reorganizing tables and furniture to my liking and according to my plan.

Believe it or not, the preparation program actually spends an entire module on the physical layout of a classroom and requires students to use an online design service to design their own. The practice was so important that we had been advised to bring and explain the design during the interview process. As I mentioned before, the classroom management portion of the program was invaluable to me so I was thankful to have a plan.

I was greeted by my closest teacher neighbor and Social Studies department chair, Mike. This younger middle-aged man had screened me over the phone and I instantly recognized his kind voice. He offered a sincere welcome and gave me a few parting instructions as I finished arranging the room and making conversation with the temporary substitute who had been one of the at least four other substitutes to tend to the class before my arrival right before Halloween.

Once I finished a quick preparation of the classroom, I made my way to the central core of the building. This area was a two-story teacher workroom filled with cubicle offices, lunch tables, and conference rooms. It was an ingenious design by Tom that maximized social interactions and gave teachers a place to work privately from their classrooms. I got in line for the photocopy machine and learned one of my first hard lessons about public schools.

There were two outdated, practically smoking off-brand copy machines, one for the lower grades and the other for junior and senior teachers. Signs about conserving paper due to budget shortages and reminders about how to unjam the dilapidated machine were posted all around. Not to be trusted with using good judgment, I entered the special pin code I was issued that would track how many copies I made and report to the secretary whether I was performing my job in an "environmentally-responsible" manner.

Once I had secured my belongings in the advised safe area, I tightened my carefully selected tie and grabbed some coffee. As the custodians, all happening to be either minorities or non-English-speaking Hispanics, sat around the lunch tables reading the local newspaper with feet comfortably propped on the tables, I made my way back to my classroom for the big moment—the students were arriving.

I hadn't really asked for a lot of information about the teacher whom I was replacing. Subtle quips and comments led me to believe something controversial had happened leading to his involuntary exit. I had never met the man and decided to completely avoid the topic and reserve judgment because it was simply none of my business. Unfortunately, not knowing what I was walking into made my first few weeks much tougher than I expected.

As I had learned during the preparation program, it was best to greet students at the door on the first day of classes. Making eye contact, making introductions, and warmly greeting them is always the best policy. Since it was my first day I decided to treat it like their first day as well. My first class began right before eight in the morning, and students trickled in until the first bell rang. This was it, our first stare down. So far, they looked terrified and I looked like the newbie I was.

As I began taking the roll, a young man pounded his fist on the door. Now, you have to understand I always lock my classroom doors. The reason I lock them is because my outlook on classroom safety changed on April 16, 2007 when a deviant killer invaded Virginia Tech (my graduate alma mater) and murdered 32 innocent and defenseless students and faculty. Though there was no policy against my locked door rule, I learned years later that it had angered many administrators. Every classroom door had full view glass beside it and every staff member used the same key to enter every classroom, so I had no hesitation.

I answered the door, and let the young man in. This young man we'll call Quamal brushed by me with his baggy blue jeans dangling around his thighs and his boxer shorts exposed front and back. He was wearing a sideways–turned baseball cap with a logo I didn't recognize, a rosary around his neck (a current gang symbol), and bulky headphones on his head. He looked back over his shoulder and inquisitively asked "Who you be?" I motioned him to his newly assigned seat as the overhead speakers came on with the morning announcements.

You can imagine my surprise when I stood up for the morning Pledge of Allegiance only to see half of the students casually talking and ignoring the world around them. The farm kids stood at attention almost uniformly with the other well-dressed White kids and two Blacks and Hispanics. I quickly got the class's attention and at least managed to settle them down enough so we could all hear the announcements that they later swear they never heard.

When the announcements concluded I began my introductory spiel and started laying out the foundation for a new beginning to the class. If you've ever seen Whoopi Goldberg in the role of a new teacher at an inner city parochial school, you can imagine the scene in my classroom. Though not nearly as hostile or stereotypical as hers, my classroom was now ground zero for my initiation as a new teacher.

Chapter Four—Walking the Walk

I was treading water. I'd been inundated with countless administrative burdens that seemed totally and completely outside the scope of my job as a teacher. In fact, I had quickly developed a rather curt response to demanding emails and phone calls from central office educrats and secretaries who made a habit of expecting teachers to do their work. Between trying to process the endless stack of requests for special education and the mounting disciplinary follow-ups, I was quite nearly drowning.

Tom and Mike were consistent in their support and encouragement, but I knew there was a learning curve I would have to conquer. Although I didn't mind fulfilling some of the same duties as I had observed my high school teachers doing, I grew increasingly annoyed at the expectations on my time. I was hired to teach children U.S. Government, period. Unfortunately, teachers in public education are forced to put their teaching on the back burner in lieu of being part time secretaries. Hiring secretaries to do secretaries' work costs money, and that isn't an option in public education. So, in typical fashion the extraordinarily high paid and underworked educrats pushed the secretarial tasks onto the faculty.

The philosophical clash between the instruction and human-centric approach of Tom and the weight being brought to bear on his teachers by the system was a constant struggle. Between counseling students, feeding students, shuttling students, and disciplining students there was not much time left for teaching students. I didn't have any illusions about the demands of the job. I knew and accepted happily the role of quasi counselor and role model. However, I openly resented the unnecessary roles of babysitter and bureaucrat for which I was not being paid.

The school system was an odd duck indeed. Even though the community was predominately rural, the school board was a mix of homespun Conservatives and idealist Liberals. This was the same school system that made national news the year I was hired for having banned the Diary of Anne Frank due to its suggestive content. The eclectic board was kept largely unapprised of the radical career educrats running the daily operations of the school division in opposition to the values and will of the public that paid their salaries.

This wholly unaccountable and extraordinarily powerful entity is the character behind what I coined years ago as an Edutocracy. All around the country, the bastions of higher education are believed to be the primary refuge for extreme progressives. The truth, however, is that the public school system is a spill over for those who either couldn't handle the demands of intellectualism or those who want to inject their progressive filth into public education.

Choosing an example to illustrate this point is like going to a library and finding an example of a book. Among the chief perpetrators of abuse against children is the state of Maryland's public school system. After illegally questioning a five year old boy in mortal terror for hours on end, he urinated all over himself before being suspended for ten days because he brought a toy cap gun on a school bus. This was only a short time after another Maryland boy became a national news story after he chewed his pop tart snack into the shape of Idaho, but was suspended because it looked like a gun. Not to be outdone, another little girl was suspended as a terrorist for talking about her toy soap bubble gun. *Tinker v. DeMoines, and* the First and Fourth Amendments all be damned, school districts around the country use their school resource police officers, rent-a-cops, and power-mad principals to censor innocent clothing, search, strip search, and interrogate children despite laws that prevent them from doing so. When confronted they cite the published policies of the school system, which in their mind supersede any and every statute and the U.S. Constitution.

In one instance, I really ruffled some feathers when I openly called one of these leftist educrats a book burner. Coincidentally, this was before I even knew about the banning of Anne Frank. The incident started when my students brought to my attention that several legitimate and family friendly websites they needed for research were being blocked by the school's IT department. The educrat's argument was that the school system was legally obligated to censor websites for sensitive subjects so that students wouldn't be exposed to inappropriate content. Although he was spot on with his statement, he was also wildly misguided in his application of the law. In fact, these students were unable to access academic and political information sources that included words like "gay, lesbian, bisexual, or transgender." I suggested, much to his chagrin, that we also burn the school's encyclopedias.

I quickly took on the persona of what was called "noncompliance." I questioned the use of my time for ancillary non-instructional tasks, and I openly took to task secretaries and administrators who lacked the academic credentials to meddle in my classroom. I did these things because I felt I had to set a standard for how I expected to be treated. I showed uncompromising kindness to everyone, but I held firm the expectation of professional courtesy I knew I had earned. Regardless of my attempts to convey kindness and preserve my integrity, I was met on all sides with overwhelming administrative intimidation and equally underwhelming support from my less than bold peers.

In most instances there is an administrative explanation behind the burden on teachers. While I and my peers were working upwards of 50 hours per week and only being paid for 35, there were countless school level and central office employees who held strict 9 to 5 workdays with quiet lunches away from their desks or out in town. I even made what I thought was a sensible argument to one of the educrats during a chance encounter on a weekend. I proposed that in light of the budgetary struggles of the system and the near to the bottom ranking of the system in teacher pay across the Commonwealth, perhaps the best and freest way to compensate people was with some flexibility and professional respect. She scoffed and walked away. Despite these extreme disparities in personnel treatment, I decided to stay focused on why I was there and that reminder sufficed to placate me for a long time.

One of the most common misconceptions about public school teachers is that they all endorse the behavior of their employers. In fact, many of us do not. I am even willing to say most of the people with which I worked would be considered dissenters. Teachers work 10 months per year with breaks for holidays. During those holidays, we plan and grade; there is little vacationing going on. We're forced by the school divisions to waste 5-7 days per year attending professional development and in-service days, all of which take the place of the school day. Believe me when I tell you that we despise these meetings as much as the public despises paying for them. During the summer we attend workshops and seminars, and then if we're lucky we get a week or two of vacation with our families. Not all of us are lemmings.

Chapter Five—The Golden Ticket

Part of teaching is said to be swallowing your pride and professional judgment for the system. Thanks partly to overzealous misapplication of the law, some of the worst abuses of teachers happen under the guise of helping needy children. One such instance, supported by dozens of subsequent experiences, forever informed my view of what are called 504 Plans, administrative modifications, and IEPs (Individualized Education Plans).

Not to be confused with actual accommodations for disabled students with physical or learning disabilities, these directives are better known among teachers as "Get out of jail free" cards. Whereas disabled students should and do receive help learning, these modified education plans are intended to ease the burden for and improve the success rate of kids who either aren't genetically predisposed to be intelligent or who simply refuse to work. I don't subscribe to the imagery of school as a jail, but an escape from responsibility is certainly an accurate description.

Akin to a golden ticket, these documents shield students from earning failing grades by requiring teachers to lower state mandated standards, often under questionable legal circumstances and the threat of disciplinary action. The plans shift accountability for student and family choices onto the classroom teacher and target any and all blame for failure as far as possible from the responsible party. The practice has gotten so out of hand that even community colleges and some institutions of higher education are relenting to these manufactured pity plans. The golden ticket follows the child to college where it is gaining traction and chipping away the integrity of a college education.

To illustrate the point, I'll share a brief story. Shortly after I began teaching I was asked to meet with a student and his parents. The student and his parents claimed that the child got too nervous while taking tests and that nervousness caused him to perform poorly. The parents requested a 504 plan that required me to send the student to an unsupervised area with other students casually talking while he took as much time as he wanted to complete the test. This example is only one of dozens I encountered in a short period.

One of the most troubling entitlements is the test reading option. Given the total disaster that is literacy education in public schools, teachers are often forced to read students' tests to them aloud and even allow them to answer aloud. As if this wasn't ridiculous enough, students even have special notes written in their files that prevent teachers from notifying parents about failing grades for fear of the child being disciplined at home. Abuse cases would explain this modification, but the practice is so overused that some students' files go so far as to bar teachers from sending progress reports and report cards home altogether. The state replaces the parents.

I was able to remain in compliance with these mandates by meeting the strict letter of the directive and compelling other teachers to do the same. For students who did not like taking notes or who claimed they could not write fast enough, I was required to provide them with lecture notes. I did exactly that. I asked for a student to volunteer to take notes for the other child. When questioned by the most radical of the assistant principals, I explained that there was no time during the school day for me to hand write the volumes of U.S. Government into lecture notes for one child. After she refused my flippant offer to photocopy years' worth of old legal pads of lecture speaker's notes, I offered to write all new notes in exchange for teaching one less class knowing she would get the point and let it drop. She did.

Measures such as these learning plans and other accountability shrinking measures for students are a component of a larger movement that has done extraordinary damage to public education and American society. Lest you think that giving free notes and unlimited test time are the extent of the requests we receive as teachers, I dedicate a later chapter to some real whoppers. If we had to assign one word to describe the disproportionate amount of money spent on faux special needs education, it'd be "boondoggle."

Chapter Six—Being Professor Lupin

Let's set the record straight before I go too far with this metaphor. By the end of my first year, my students and I had drawn uncanny parallels between our school and its population in comparison to the setting and characters of J.K. Rowling's Harry Potter book series. At first I was worried that the story would make me look like an overzealous fan at a comic book convention, but the truth is that my students were spot on. Allegories and parallels are often the best way to tell a new story.

By the end of that year I was referred to, colloquially, as "Lupin." Remus Lupin is one of Rowling's teacher characters. The character has an uncompromising love for his students. He is fiercely independent in his dealings with authority. Moreover, he takes very seriously a holistic approach to education that nurtures the students' personal development as well as their academic training. Even though he maintains a close-knit group of friends, he is often ostracized by colleagues for his roguishness. In many ways, Lupin is seen as much as a parental figure than a teacher.

One of Tom's brightest instructional designs was his insertion of a flexible window of time into the school's daily schedule. This half hour time was used for remediation, fine arts practices, club meetings, administrative tasks, etc. When students didn't have those tasks, the expectation was that they be in a consistent and supervised area with a teacher. After realizing they could find a short period of peace, my classroom became this "safe" space.

Although I always had work to do, this was one of my favorite portions of the day. One of the joys of teaching is watching young people grow and mature into adults and convincing ourselves that somehow we contributed a little bit. As a very young teacher, I was only five or six years older than most of my senior students. At the same time, I have a presence that exudes a sober and steady temperament. This balance some- how sent the message to students that we could get along well — and we did.

Constantly tending the necessary precautions to avoid impro- priety, I intentionally made a connection with some of the kids. I think it's fair to say many teachers do. Whether we were talk- ing about or watching a clip of one of our favorite television shows like "Glee" or having a more serious discussion about college, the room was always glowing with a group of students who were comfortable letting their typically guarded personali- ties show through. Admittedly there were times when I let a minor curse word go unchecked or less than mature comment slip by, but I am confident that there was a balance of life les- sons and reality that made the whole atmosphere work. There were points when students from other classes and students I didn't know were constantly in my classroom because they told me they felt safe. To this day, I can't replace the joy that gave me.

Being Remus Lupin also had its tougher moments though. At one point I found myself in the confidence of a student who had recently discovered she was pregnant. Another hard cir- cumstance happened when I was approached by a young woman who felt the need to tell me she was bisexual. By the end of my three years behind the iron curtain, I became the leading confidant and advocate for students struggling with their sexuality and others who had been cast out by their peers. In all of these situations I had to walk a fine line.

Between mandatory reporting activities like self-abuse and abuse at home to other precarious positions when students just needed that safe place, I constantly maintained a dialogue with the counseling office. Now that I look back at those tougher conversations, I wouldn't do them any differently. After all, I took on the teacher's job, and that role means more today than ever because kids are lacking role models at home and in the community. While I certainly valued the bonds I built with my kids, I also noticed the growing grumblings of other staff members who resented my connection with students. According to some, I undermined their authoritarian classroom management style.

My classroom wasn't like most. We all faced each other, and we all knew each other's names. I take the unorthodox view that I couldn't care less whether the kids called me Dr. or Mr. In fact; I encouraged them to call me by my first name. I did so because I needed to send a deeper message to them. I had been at the receiving end of egomaniacs who demanded respect for no other reason than because of their haughty titles. I even knew a guy who faked his credentials from a university in the Deep South just so that he would get the respect. I wanted to earn my students' respect because of my expertise in my field and my treatment of them as human beings. Despite the naysayers out there, this policy was a whopping success for me, and about three quarters of the kids ended up calling me by my academic title of Dr. or just "Mr. E" even though they knew they didn't need to. For the rest, it was Lupin, Pippin, or "hey you."

Chapter Seven — I am Harrison Bergeron

One of the short films I consistently share with my students is a film entitled "2081." This film adaption of Kurt Vonnegut's short story titled "Harrison Bergeron" is a fictional futuristic story about the dangers of radical egalitarianism. The story follows a character who lives under the tyrannical regime of a bureaucrat Hell-bent on making everyone equal.

Those who are beautiful are forced to wear masks. Smart people have to wear noise-making devices in their ears to prevent them from concentrating too hard and taking unfair advantage of their brains. Strong people wear weights on their arms and legs to make them as weak as everyone else. Like any other experiment in socialism, everyone is equally miserable.

Students have a tendency to rebel against these ideas. In fact, I've had students really get angry after the film and discussion because they live in a lesser fanatic version of Harrison Bergeron's world. I often answer their frustration with a quote from a favorite President of mine, Calvin Coolidge, who said during his booming economy and culture of the 1920s that we shouldn't expect to raise up the weak by tearing down the strong.

You should know that despite my focus on ability levels, I am not a one level teacher. Although I was hired to and primarily taught advanced placement, college level, and honors students, I insisted on keeping one general or average level class per semester. I made the decision that I never wanted to forget the extent to which average level students still need great teachers that will challenge them fairly. To that end, I taught a general level class my entire time behind the iron curtain, and I wouldn't trade that experience for the world.

This business of equality in outcome is a symptom of a larger disease. One of the ways this disease manifests itself is through what are called "differentiated or tiered classrooms." Partly as obfuscations for lack of resources, these classes are the new normal for most of public education. Gifted and advanced students are mixed with average and learning disabled students under the failed notion that the lower achievers will rise to greatness. In fact, the only measurable effect from this practice is the uniformed mediocrity of the whole lot.

Only five to six years removed from high school at the time, I noticed everything was different. The days of tracking students by academic level were gone. The long standing and academically sound practice of grouping students by ability level and then allowing improving students to move up in level was nixed on account of its negative impact on children's self-esteem. Instead of having remedial, career, honors, and gifted levels of classes, educrats coopted scheduling counselors (formerly known as guidance counselors) and radical leftist administrators into combining the students into one central mess.

The results of the practice are deeply troubling, almost nauseating. In the same room as the Ivy League-bound wonder student is an equally kind and hard-working student who only reads at the level of a middle school student. In the classroom of 30 students, the teacher is forced to spend his time remediating the failing student instead of enriching the brilliant student. Not only are both children done an injustice, but the teacher grows increasingly frustrated with a system that confines him to failure.

As a practical act of heresy, not even the most rogue educators are willing to challenge this practice for fear of being labeled some typical expected slur such as "arrogant, racist, sexist, backward, oppressive, etc." So, in typical fashion, and fully unaware of the storm I'd end up causing, I raised my voice.

When four general level students enrolled in my college level government and politics class I knew something would have to give. As an offering of the local community college and because I had the academic credentials required to do it, I taught a college credit bearing class to advanced high school students. Unfortunately, the school district's policy of "Open Enrollment" prevented teachers from screening students for their reading and writing ability before they signed up for the class.

After a week of offering these students every extra resource in the world (including my extra time), I finally referred them to guidance to be switched out of the class because they were failing. In fact, two of the students had trouble reading at a middle school level. As was the normal practice division wide, I sent out notices of concern to the parents regarding their student's performance. After all, I wanted the students to succeed and knew from their performance they had bitten off more than they could chew.

In short order, the gates of judgment opened upon me like a ton of bricks that could speak insulting words. I was harangued for not lowering the college mandated standards to meet the low ability level of the students. I was called insensitive and instructionally deficient for not slowing down the entire class to cater to these four students. In fact, I was verbally reprimanded for even using the expression "slow down" because that may have been an implicit insult to lower achievers.

Most nastily and hurtfully, I was called, by the radical egalitarian assistant principal, named Ethel, a racist and a sexist because the four students happened to be Black females. Ethel threw this epithet at me like a dagger despite the fact that my two highest performers in that particular class were Black students. This middle aged White woman seethed at me as if I had committed a personal offense. She cemented her anger by remarking that I reminded her of teachers she had encountered who used the code "LBG" to signal a loud, Black, girl. Only later did I learn that her obsession with race in school was a larger and deeper issue of concern that had landed her in some heat on more than one occasion.

The parents of these students did not want them in a college level class, and the girls tried to switch after my recommendation, but their requests were mitigated by the intervention of the chief of social justice who also happened to be the head guidance counselor. Only after forcibly involving the college and threatening to decertify the course as college level did the administrators relent. As in most cases, the instructional experts are the teachers, but our voices are silenced whenever our judgment interferes with the widget assembly line.

In one of the broadest examples of real damage being done to our struggling students, especially racial minorities and students with behavioral issues, I bring your attention to graduation behind the iron curtain.

Chapter Eight—Commencement versus Graduation

At a time when schools and school districts are being held financially responsible by the Federal government for failing students, the edutocracy has practically perfected a new way to dodge accountability. I introduce to you the terms "modified diploma" and "commencement." Not to be confused with an education, a diploma is a piece of paper valued only by what went into it. Most students get diplomas, but fewer earn an education.

You see, calling the ceremony a graduation would imply that the people walking across the stage were graduating from high school. The catch here is that not all of the students walking during the ceremony were actually graduating, hence the term commencement. Some were commencing to college and careers while others were just commencing their failed behinds off the premises. By avoiding the liability of a graduation, the educrats had already covered one base. However there was one more issue for which they had to concoct an administrative solution.

One would think graduating or commencing from high school comes along with a diploma. However, seeing no place for logic in public education there was no reason to start here. Students received diplomas, modified diplomas, and certificates. While students who actually managed to receive (earned or otherwise) passing grades received a diploma, they weren't the only ones to do so. Take, for example, a student named Sally. Sally could have failed her standardized tests even though she passed her classes, or vice versa. She could have even passed all but one class and simply "tried hard." The fix for

Sally and countless others is to suddenly discover they have a need for accommodation (the Golden Ticket). Such a learning impairment would justify the issuance of a modified diploma — a legally recognized high school diploma implying all of the same social and career legitimacy as the brightest student in the ceremony. To make matters more frustrating, there is a third option for walking across the stage.

Sally's friend John may have been given a certificate. Not to be confused with a diploma or modified diploma, the certificate is exactly what it sounds like. Toward the end of the year it was obvious to everyone John was not going to pass. Seeing that John was in his second attempt at the twelfth grade or simply disinterested in school, he was given another opportunity to have his parents take a picture of him wearing a cap and gown. Before the ceremony, a secretary would print out some generic certificate of completion on a piece of fancy paper and hand it to John during the ceremony instead of a diploma. Don't worry though, the certificate was inside of a pretty diploma folder just like every other child so that no one would know he was different.

At the end of my first year teaching high school I was changed forever. Most of the micro level changes were positive, but my view of public education was exponentially worse. To top off the bad news, Tom was leaving us. He was making a family and career transition away from our school, and all of us were left wondering what was next. Despite his best attempts at shielding his teachers from some of the more draconian policies being forced upon the school district by its central office managers, our school was now a target for major changes.

My admiration for Tom was informed, but so was my limited professional criticism. Sometimes appearing, incorrectly, to be aloof after years of management and principal burnout, Tom had left the school with a few problems. Though none of them were serious and very few were directly his fault, the school was certain to change. Violence among misbehaved and parentless minority students had garnered the attention of the local news, and the district's mandated admittance of a violent criminal student seriously injured a faculty member.

The loose and guided developmental focus Tom had instilled into his staff was too humanitarian for the powers that be. Not to be confused with passivism, Tom used discipline appropriately and expected his faculty to do the same. Moreover, academics and performing arts were at an above average level of achievement and on the rise when he departed. What the school needed, and I think Tom would agree, was a little tightening of the belt and a refresher on structure.

The reason Tom is held in such high regard by teachers is because he established a culture that left teachers as independent as was reasonably possible. Although he made no secret of his devout politically Liberal beliefs, he also didn't hold my equally fervent Conservative Libertarianism against me. I was allowed to follow my philosophy of education in my classroom as was every other teacher. Although politics may not seem to matter in a school atmosphere, I learned as time went by that politics drives practically every decision that is made.

Never before or since had I seen students so admire a school principal. From hugs in the hallway to high fives from every other kid that passed by, Tom connected with those kids. On more than once occasion, Tom would see a kid who had forgotten lunch money or was just hungry and he'd reach into his pocket and quietly hand the kid money for lunch or a snack. He even bought one of the art student's paintings as a sign to her that he was proud of her beautiful work. That kind of responsible mentorship is a hard find today.

Needless to say, graduation that year was a tough experience for everyone. However, I didn't realize exactly how tough it would be until I started entering my final grades for the spring semester. Upon realizing that a handful of students had chosen to fail my class, I reported their grades accordingly. I felt comfortable that I had offered opportunities above and beyond anything I was required to do and given the failing students ample opportunities to succeed. Mike reminded me of something I will never forget. He said, "Brian we can lead them to water and put lead weights around their neck to push them into the water, but we can't force them to drink." I took that advice to heart and still do.

Chapter Nine—Rotten to the Core

At this point you've undoubtedly heard this reframing of the new Common Core state standards. Worn out or not, critics chose an apt name for this abomination. In the past, states and localities have managed their own curriculum and instructional practices. However, as with most things that work too well, we allow the government to come in and destroy it. Hailed as a revolutionary step toward standardizing quality among all of the public schools, the CCSS are a set of concocted goals and guidelines put forth upon the states. As of the time of this publication, only four states have refused to accept CCSS: Virginia, Texas, Nebraska, and Alaska.

Although proponents refuse to acknowledge it, CCSS dictate curriculum to public schools in such a way that local school boards have to abdicate authority over their state Constitutional duties. While pushing basic Algebra all of the way into high schools, collecting highly inappropriate and intimate data about children and their families, and stripping away the instructional prerogative from teachers. The supporters will say that the CCSS simply set a general set of benchmarks that identify where students ought to be at each grade level. The truth couldn't be any more different.

In order to meet the standards and benchmarks put forth by CCSS, school systems have to subscribe to curricula that rewrite American history into a pro-Palestinian, ultra secular, revisionist history nightmare. Instead of describing the Islamic terrorist attacks of September 11, 2001 as such, CCSS suggest a tiny paragraph that mentions the events as a "human tragedy that resulted from a clash of cultures after years of American influence abroad." The heroes children are taught to admire are not George Washington, Harriet Tubman, and Neil Armstrong. Kids are instead taught to look to people such as Karl Marx, Mao Zedong, and Malcolm X.

The indirect assault on teachers via the establishment of "Professional Learning Communities" is an equally threatening aspect of CCSS. Normally, teachers write their own tests and class materials and, without school board appeal, have ultimate grading authority in the classroom. Under CCSS, teachers are forced to adopt collaborative team-driven materials. They have to negotiate with their peers to write common quizzes, tests, activities, and grading rubrics. All sense of instructional liberty is stripped from teachers who believe strongly in essay tests, fill-in-the-blank tests, and reading quizzes while the teachers who espouse multiple-option tests, suggested homework, and creative math are allowed to dumb down the entire school. This interference by educrats into the classrooms of teachers who are otherwise acting professionally and generally autonomously as education professionals is the most sacrilegious affront to teachers yet.

Lest you mistakenly think the CCSS are only opposed by the Conservatives and Libertarians of America, take a look at the concerns of run-of-the-mill independents and moderates, and you'll see they are equally offended. The thinking and scheming of a handful of radical educrats is being forced upon the other 98 percent of America in a way that defies our system of Federalism and the forgotten sanctity of the tenth Amendment. Before you decide whether to allow your child to attend a public school in any state, ask yourself this: Are you okay with your child being asked "Have you ever seen daddy hit mommy?" or "Do your mom and dad keep a gun in your house?" or "Have you ever seen your mom and dad take a lot of pills?" If that doesn't scare you, then you're a fool. The four hold out states are not exempt from this threat. Radical educrats in Texas are trying to institute CCSS under a different name CSCOPE; Virginia (the founder of CCSS) rejected the CCSS but is slowly sneaking the CCSS into its statutes via the Virginia Department of Education. Educrats are flexing their muscle through the power of the state executive branch in clear defiance of the will of the state legislature in Richmond.

Common Core introduces the most unprecedented level of Federal intervention into education since Lyndon Johnson's disastrous Elementary and Secondary Education Act. After receiving countless millions of dollars of support from the Bill and Malinda Gates Foundation through an organization called "Achieve," President Obama and many Liberal Democrats hail CCSS as the new gold standard of education. Despite that vocal support, teachers, administrators, and lawmakers are chipping away at CCSS in their respective states every day. The danger to the public school system is grave.

Chapter Ten—Sea Change

Have you ever heard someone reminisce about the good old days? The problem is that we barely ever notice the good old days until they are gone. We're so used to complaining that every day is hard or stressful. Well, following the end of my first year behind the iron curtain I became one of those people in a hurry.

The tricky part about talking about being disabled is that it can appear self-serving. At the same time, there are a lot of handicapped people who share my sentiment and stay silent so much that we inadvertently marginalize ourselves. Keeping the excuses short and the hard work coming is the best way to balance out the bitching. This story about the sea change is made of a few waves, and the first happened exactly like being hit by an unexpected wave on an otherwise peaceful beach.

Tom's replacement had been chosen practically overnight. Unlike most civilized school systems, the faculty of our school had absolutely no input in his hiring. Only one level above the student sheep, we were the border collies nipping at their heels to stay in line. The new herder came in with a flurry of local hubbub. The guy they chose had briefly visited the school during the interview process and looked on with total disdain and disgust at what he saw.

As an added insult, the faculty found out about the selection of the new principal via the local newspaper along with everyone else. We were told all about his state principal of the year award and his military style management. Upon further research, we started to get a better idea of what was coming. One of my colleagues was intuitive enough to call the new principals former high school and make some general inquires about his reputation among teachers. Along with an extraordinarily high attrition rate among teachers, the man was known for his abrasiveness and political prowess. That fear and influence was made obvious when the teachers with which my colleague inquired actually called their former boss to let him know we were checking into him.

Having learned about her experience, I have to share a story that will leave you dumbstruck. One of the responsibilities of a building principal is to handle the initial intake and adjudication of requests for accommodation under the Americans with Disabilities Act. In a nutshell, this law signed by the first President Bush requires employers to grant flexibility to employees who are otherwise qualified and able to do their job with reasonable modifications to accommodate their disability. The ADA makes it illegal for an employer to inquire into or reject candidates based on their disability or deny a request for accommodation without offering an equally helpful counterproposal. In essence, this law allows disabled people to make an honest wage and be productive members of society instead of living on the dole as victims.

One such request frequently comes from new mothers. When women choose to breastfeed, that process doesn't happen according to class bell schedules. They need, and are legally entitled to, a private and sanitary place to pump their breasts. Unfortunately, this particular colleague of mine enjoyed no such flexibility.

After making the request to pump her breasts during the day as needed, Jane's request was met with a denial by the new principal and his brash counterpart in the human resources office. There was a concern that her need to pump her breasts was too unpredictable and would be a distraction for her students should she need to excuse herself from class for a few minutes. Instead of simply working out a coverage option for her, she was directed that she needed to schedule her breast pumping sessions on an approved administrative schedule. When she refused and enlisted the assistance of the teachers' union, she was met with hostility and subtle public embarrassment, but ultimately did come to a less than amicable agreement.

I only became aware of her experience after my own troubling time receiving coverage under the ADA. One of the most serious parts of my long scientifically named neurological affliction is the loss of mobility and physical dexterity as the day passes. In spite of proper medicinal treatment and lifestyle management, my active day essentially ends after lunch time. After about eight hours of being up and about, my body quickly drains down for a nap and a long evening before being ready to go again the next day. I often liken it to living with an alkaline battery in a lithium world.

As a teacher, this schedule works pretty well. I can teach and be active during nearly all of the school day and then reserve grading and planning for my lesser mobile and active period in the afternoons. The first year with Tom had been well-planned and the issue never arose after our initial discussion of my class schedule. I taught my classes, did my administrative tasks, and then left for the day unless there was an important function I needed to attend. It was the kind of treatment that any professional should expect from their employer. It was also the humanity that Tom showed his staff. There wasn't even a need to formally go through the paperwork juggle. That all changed with the sea.

I had started looking for a new faculty position in another division closer to home. Although I enjoyed the time I had spent, I could feel the tide coming in, and the daily hour long drive had gotten stale and expensive. I was blessed to interview for a position fifteen minutes from home and receive an offer shortly thereafter. Unfortunately, the teacher contract trap and the irrational stubbornness of the new sheep herder blocked my transfer. I didn't learn until months later he had directly intervened to prevent me from leaving. When I realized the move wasn't going to happen and I needed to find a way to safeguard my health against a protracted school day, I did what any responsible person would do—I followed the law.

Having used the ADA once before to secure a modified work schedule with my previous employer when I was a government contractor, I was relatively familiar with the process. I provided my request, my medical documentation, and an offer for an open dialogue. In response, I was hit full force with an administrative wave that knocked me flat on my face.

What you have to understand is that public school divisions operate like fiefdoms. As I documented before, they have extraordinary amounts of power accumulated over decades and the publicly-funded legal resources to write their own ticket. Educrats cling to this power like life itself and will fight to the bitter and nasty end to keep it. Moreover, they'll openly seek to destroy anyone who challenges them. The iron curtain really became clear during this summer.

Chapter Eleven — Colonel Custer and the Teachers' Union

George Armstrong Custer was a decorated Civil War hero of the Union whose medals were outshined only by his massive ego and propensity for bullheadedness. His unfounded high opinion of himself ultimately led to his embarrassing defeat and untimely death at the Battle of the Little big Horn at the hands of a female American Indian. Although I was well apprised of the story of Colonel Custer, I had no idea he'd been reincarnated as my new principal.

If Yosemite Sam had a twin, it was my new principal. This Blackberry-wielding educrat may as well been wearing a saber and a blue coat. After the chief of social justice and Mike failed to accommodate my illness and I had exhausted all of my informal attempts to correct their mistake, I had to schedule a meeting with Colonel Custer.

When I showed up to the school during the summer break, I was immediately surprised that the building wasn't being climate controlled. After all, the school system could save a buck fifty by letting this brand new multimillion building fill with the damaging humidity and heat of a Virginia summer. I walked back to Custer's office, which was freshly redecorated with self-accolades and the hallmarks of an anal retentive administrator, and there he was. Only, there was another man sitting there too. The brash and unprofessional human resources educrat I had encountered the day of my hiring was sitting there with legs crossed and teeth gritted.

After making introductions and a little polite small talk about the weather, Colonel Custer began to speak in his trademark nasal and choppy Southern drawl. As a measure to cover his liabilities, Custer had brought in the director of the division's human resources office, Butch. As the three of us talked and I explained my request for accommodation, I knew from the start I was doing what my grandmother used to call "making an argument to the ass end of a cow." The two men had already decided how they were going to adjudicate the matter, and even though I wanted to remain hopeful I think I knew it was a waste of time.

To my surprise at the time, Custer cut a deal with me. In exchange for my provisional willingness to teach late afternoon classes in the Fall, he would work with the scheduler to make changes to the Fall if possible, but absolutely in time for the Spring semester. In my mind, this was a fair compromise. Even though I was entitled to much more under the law, I thought that this initial act of good faith compromise was a positive way to make a first impression with my new boss. In one of the few times in my entire life I can say this, I was a total sucker. Throughout the fall, no such changes were made or even discussed. In their minds, I'd been temporarily placated like a whining child. In one of the most pointless and enlightening acts of my professional teaching career, I contacted the teachers' union.

Up to this point I may have sounded union friendly. As a lifelong critic of the viral nature of labor unions, I hadn't initially joined. However, after convincing myself that I would only join for the protection of the union against liability issues, I bit the bullet and made a deal with the devil. Not a day went by that I didn't regret that decision. The use of the school system's email server by the Democrat union to spread political propaganda sent me off the deep end on more than one occasion. The cliquish nature of the union and non-union faculty was also palpable. Even in the right-to-work state of Virginia, labor unions appear to members to offer them protection from abusive employers and group negotiated discounts on goods and services. I essentially held in my disgust and forked over the hundreds of dollars just hoping I would never need to interact with them.

Eventually though, I couldn't fight the human resource battle over my disability alone. I contacted the union representative and scheduled a meeting with her. At the time I did not expect to have what little hope for unions I'd retained destroyed all at once. After explaining back the portions of the ADA about which I was already a near-expert, the union rep informed me that the best course of action was to write a nice letter to the human resources director requesting his reconsideration.

After literally weeks of exchanging pointless letters that were hand-delivered by Colonel Custer to my classroom on official school system letterhead, I was denied any meaningful accommodation whatsoever. The response of the union rep, the state level union officers and lawyers, and the national level member services office was all the same—too bad, so sad. I was told to expect not to have my division teaching contract renewed due to my challenging of the system and that I was essentially out of luck. The same organization that has, on several very public occasions, moved heaven and Earth to help its members couldn't [wouldn't] negotiate a settlement between me and Butch.

After this whole cabal had come to an unproductive end I made two vows to myself: 1) cancel my membership to the Democrat political advocacy teacher union, and 2) make every possible effort to remind Colonel Custer and Butch of their lies as often and as loudly as possible. The former took until the end of the member contract year (the NEA locks you into a contract), and the latter was and is an ongoing hobby of mine. One of the most troubling and true memories I have of this experience is this. At one point I simply had to threaten to resign. Butch, without hesitating for a moment, said "That's fine, Brian. There are a hundred guys right behind you waiting for your job." And when I mentioned legal action on a separate occasion, I was reminded by a third party that the school system's view on lawsuits by teachers is that they cost tens of thousands of dollars, and teachers simply don't have the resources to fight a public entity in court without going bankrupt in the process. They're immune.

Chapter Twelve—Eating Crow and Concrete

I needed to focus on great teaching. After all, I knew I was an accomplished expert in my academic field as well as the classroom. At least, that was the pep talk I gave myself on the mornings when the new burdens of Colonel Custer's regime weighed most heavily on my shoulders. I knew there was solace to be found in effective instruction and positive student interactions, and that is exactly what I found.

I was heading into the Spring semester, and that meant a new set of faces. On the semester block system, students took one set of classes in the Fall and another in the Spring with AP classes spanning the whole year. Since my schedule hadn't been fixed I was stuck teaching two general level classes, one of which was in the afternoon. I didn't mind teaching one general level class, but to do more than that was a waste of my credentials and not fair to the kids. Nonetheless, I smiled like a good soldier and did it anyway.

Going into the afternoon class I had been warned by my peers that a couple of the kids were a particular problem in terms of their behavior. One boy had such an awful reputation that he'd been regularly kicked out of school for fighting and other serious misbehavior. He was open about the fact that he smoked marijuana, and he often came to school with the lingering effects of that activity apparent. His previous semester's teacher had warned me that he was unmanageable, defiant, and intimidating.

I have a strict policy about giving each student a fresh start every day they walk into my classes. Whatever poor choices they may before won't affect my treatment of them regarding discipline. Similarly, I generally disregard any and all warnings from other teachers about how bad or good a student is until I've had the chance to meet and work with the student myself. This policy of mine especially pertained to students like Titus.

Titus scared the devil out of me. He had more tattoos and tough guy muscles than I would dare tangle with. He had a serious demeanor and deep voice that sounded like a man of 30 instead of an 18 year old high school student. He regularly dressed in the style of his peers with his jeans below his crotch and a swagger that appeared to be a mix of bowel discomfort and loafing. By this point I had learned a lot about the culture of the kids I was teaching. I was more familiar with the slang and the undercurrent of language that makes the difference between understanding the kids instead of just talking at them.

This language helped me a lot with Titus. For the first few days, he lived up to his reputation. He was loud and disruptive at the same time he was refusing to even write his name on a piece of paper. I picked up on his cues and already knew how I'd have to connect with him. Titus didn't have a man who was worth a damn in his life. I didn't know it at the time, but his only parental figure was his mother. Unlike many of the minority students I encountered, Titus actually respected his mom. She wore the pants in the house and she supervised his grades and behavior the best she could. In fact, as tough as Titus was he always dreaded a teacher calling his mom because he feared disappointing her as much as he wanted to avoid being punished.

There is something about looking in someone's eyes when you speak to them that has incredible value. Regardless of the silly culture cops who advise against making eye contact for fear of offense, there is a connection that is only possible when two people are actually having a verbal and body language conversation. Titus knew I was going to get on him about something. He stayed after class as if he knew I wanted to talk with him or yell at him like his other teachers in the past. Instead, I just asked him if he wanted a Coke.

You see, there are few problems in life that can't be solved over a cold Coca-Cola. Titus and I sat down at a table in the classroom. I had taken off my tie and relaxed a bit after the bell ended the day. Titus looked at me as if I had grown a third eye because he didn't understand what was going on. I looked at Titus and asked him to tell me about himself.

After a little hesitation, he told me a little about his family and his interests. I encouraged him to keep talking, and he eventually moved on to how he likes to make people laugh and doesn't like to be embarrassed. He talked about joining the military as an option after high school or maybe even becoming a mechanic because he really enjoyed working on cars. That was really all I wanted to know, and after thanking him for sticking around I wished him a good day and he went home.

The next day I saw something change. Titus came into class a little faster and played around a little less. He didn't yell when he spoke, and he actually half paid attention to what I was teaching. I took what I could get from him for the next few days while constantly giving him more leeway to express himself. This class happened at about the same time as a prominent news story about a controversial shooting. That current event suddenly caught Titus's interest, and he and the rest of his peers talked about it as a class.

Of course kids are still kids most of the time so I had to play referee now and then, but I noticed afterward that this was the first time Titus had not interrupted my class a single time. He had not only participated, but he also turned in the assignment for the day. Granted, it was awful, but this was the first time he actually engaged with me. What happened next is one of the stories that teachers cherish their whole career.

We were a couple of months into the term at this point and Titus had raised his low F score to a solid D. Although his progress wasn't steady by any means, it was still a huge step for this kid. I asked Titus a question during class, and I nearly choked when answered me with a calm "Yes, sir." To this day I don't know what lit the bulb, but Titus turned into a totally different kid. He started improving his grades again, and the teachers from his other classes remarked positively about his behavior in their classes. Titus kept his classmates settled with a healthy dose of "Stop talking when Erskine is talking; it's rude."

This trouble filled boy I met in January was almost a different person. He stopped giving the public free view of his underwear, and he started treating the females in class like people instead of objects from a rap video. He greeted me every day and wasn't afraid to say hello around his friends in the hallway. That tough persona he used to protect himself from being embarrassed and the great but ill-timed sense of humor had both turned into decently channeled attributes of a young man.

I may never know exactly what Titus was thinking, but I have some theories. I treated him like a human being. He knew I wasn't going to hold grudges or cut him unfair breaks. I gave him every bit of freedom I could including letting him get up and walk around a little and even sit next to his best friend, but I made him earn all of it. I didn't want Titus to stop being himself or to trade in his personality to be compliant. I did want him to find a way to be himself without setting his life up as yet another wasted opportunity.

Titus ended up graduating because he earned his grades in my class and others. I didn't keep in touch with him directly, but I was fortunate enough to bump into his mom at the grocery store months later. She said she had ended up talking Titus into attending a couple of classes at the community college so he could stay engaged with school. She reported that he'd come home one day in a bit of a snit because one of his professors had assigned him a short essay. He remarked to his mom that "This guy wants me to write about a bunch of stuff just like Erskine did last year. Thank God I saved stuff from his class because he told me college would be like this." I let that bookend serve as crow for the folks who said Titus was a lost cause.

****

The eating concrete half of this chapter is far less fun to recount. Since I wasn't receiving any accommodation from the school system to help me work around my disease, I pretty much had to tough it out. The long schedule took its toll on me both physically and mentally. By the latter half of the Spring semester, I had become increasingly reliant on medicine to keep me going, and I had built up an unhealthy tolerance to the others. I had turned my planning period into part naptime and part grading so I could get through the day. Since I always enjoyed and looked forward to eating lunch with kids who would hang out in my classroom, I stayed mentally engaged constantly.

My final class of the day was a very small group of about 12 students. In fact, it shouldn't have been a class at all because they could have been absorbed into others. However, the scheduling folks had selected the most difficult behavioral cases and academic failures and combined them into a class just for me. Whether because they knew I could handle it or because they didn't know what else to do with the kids I'll never know. I was well aware that certain teachers had reputations for being able to succeed with tough cases so they often were dumped on accordingly.

One particular afternoon I had really overspent my energy. On top of that, my classroom was unusually hot. I had asked multiple times that day and the day before for the facilities folks to rectify the problem. One of the most burdensome complications of the disease is that my body struggles to regulate temperature. Once it's overheated it can take hours to cool down and, in the process, take me out of commission for 12-24 hours. I had stayed for a faculty meeting the day before and been waning for a couple of days. Despite sleeping and the meds, I had finally exhausted my body to a point where I was walking on a cane 24/7 instead of the normal day here or there. We were reviewing for an upcoming test in this small class, and I knew something didn't feel right. The kids had asked me several times if I was okay. By that time we were practically a family, and they knew exactly what was normal and not. Moreover, I always tried to make the kids feel comfortable asking me about the disease as a way to make them less apprehensive.

I was already beyond the regular medicine regimen for the day, but I had ninety minutes left where I needed to be up and about. The temperature in the room was well over 80 degrees — well outside my tolerance. Playing review games on the Smartboard in my class is a very engaging activity where there is no lull. I was about a quarter of the way through the mock "Jeopardy" game and I started to feel a creepy and steady type of dizziness. Sitting down, drinking a Coke, and taking a break didn't seem to have any effect at all. My blood pressure was next to nil, and I could feel it.

I walked over to the door which was about five feet from the Smartboard. The kids were in the process of writing their final trivia answers when I stepped into the hall and leaned against the doorframe to get some fresher air. About that time I don't exactly remember what happened.

I woke up in the floor of the hallway. I had face planted into the floor sometime after letting go of the doorframe. On one side of me were my cane and the book I was holding. On the other side were a spilled mug of soda and the shattered mug. A piece of the mug was in my hand and there was a bit of blood around the puddle of soda and on my arm. I remember my head felt as if had been hit by Rocky Balboa and my legs were shaking violently.

Chapter Thirteen — Bedside Manner

I waited for what seemed an eternity, drifting in and out of lucidness, while the best school nurse in the world and some of my peers stood by. One of them held my head still so that the convulsions didn't do more damage. Students were all ordered back into the classrooms to avoid a panic. Ethel and Colonel Custer hovered around like vultures.

When the ambulance arrived, I was seriously convulsive but more lucid. My body temperature had reached just shy of 105 degrees. The EMTs packed ice packs around me for the short 5 mile drive, and I didn't really know what to think about my predicament. I was over an hour from home and the nearest relative and about to enter a hospital that would struggle to compete with Dr. Quinn the Medicine Woman.

The gurney made its way inside with me in a decrepit mess along for the ride. For a guy who typically carries himself with a great deal of pride and decorum, this was not my most shining moment. The triage nurses, or secretaries maybe, asked me about allergies and medications. Equally as fast they asked me who was the responsible party. Obviously it was the workers' compensation plan for the school system. Not far behind, Custer and the school hall monitor, Jack, tagged along.

My wife had been alerted via the school's phone tree by a rude and demanding phone call from the chief of social justice/guidance and scheduling educrat. I can only imagine what kind of fear that kind of phone call must cause; I only hope I never have to experience it. So my support system was on her way and I was stuck in a podunk hospital room with a man I detested and another who was just trying to be nice. Mike was there quickly as well and sat by my bedside, officially being the only person welcome in the room. It's amazing how much peace a Christian man can bring to a tough situation. I think this comfort was also accompanied by some context because a similar but less serious heat related incident had occurred my first year when Mike didn't heed my warning on a hot day.

Colonel Custer sat there whistling spit through his teeth and chatting me up like we were in a hair salon. The continual promises to see to it I was taken care of and the apologies for the heat in my classroom were about as empty as my body felt at the moment. My body was starting the cooling down process, and along with that came a fast and hard kind of fatigue. The physical exhaustion was so intense that it was a chore to keep my eyes open or speak. I had plowed into a concrete wall at full speed and just started feeling it.

Now, I wouldn't dare generalize all marriages. However, I can tell you a little about mine. We've been together since we were sophomores in high school and our worlds revolve around each other. Marrying your best friend is one of the best opportunities ever. Sarah has a full time job keeping watch over me as I try to teach, manage the disease, and live a little. In her free time she has her own high profile full time career and her own interests to pursue. Few people outside spouses know the unfiltered version of their significant other. This day was different.

If facial expression, body language, and general demeanor could send a message, Sarah walked into that hospital room like a petite high-heel wearing freight train bound and determined to get to me. I wouldn't have wanted to get in her way, and no one else did either.

As the nurses and doctors were doing EKGs and other tests, she clearly dismissed the vultures out of the room like Meryl Streep in "The Devil Wears Prada" and gave a warm thank you to Mike. When I was finally able to see her still face for a moment I was pretty surprised. One would expect tears or nervousness, but when I saw her powerful brown eyes looking at me she was as solid as a rock. I think that was the first deep breath I had taken in a couple of hours.

The rest of the evening was predictable. My folks were there, the kids were calling, and one was thankfully able to get in to see me. The medical doctors, as much as medicine is a science I suppose, diagnosed me as having collapsed due to heat exhaustion, physical overexertion, and dangerously low blood pressure. The convulsions were apparently a defense mechanism for expelling heat, and had I not been treated sooner I may have had permanent injury. I was blessed to be done with the whole mess and just wanted to sleep.

If only I had been so lucky.

Chapter Fourteen—Fool Me Once

I took the customary couple of days to recuperate. Since I was always focused on the teaching I was able to sneak past Sarah to send in lesson plans and a bunch of information to the substitute. I made it back in on Monday of the following week ready to start another week in paradise.

I received a bunch of kind cards and notes from peers and the kids. One of the boys to whom I affectionately referred to as "Opie" due to his striking resemblance to Ron Howard was waiting for me with a new coffee cup to replace the one I'd shattered during his class. In fact, that whole class had made a beautiful jumbo sized card. Later on I learned that I had excused Titus from class to use the restroom before I collapsed. When he returned to see me there he dispatched one kid to get help and literally guarded me in the hallway until help arrived. Titus was a great kid.

Things went pretty much back to normal. We jumped back into class with both feet because the AP exams were right around the corner, and the seniors were getting the graduation itch. Colonel Custer and the maintenance baboons came by my classroom to examine the temperature issue only to conclude that there was no problem. The maintenance educrat in charge informed me he had no documentation to regulate my room's temperature differently than the division-mandated temperature. I ended up having to contact the Central Planning office and speak to Butch pretty incredulously about what had just happened days prior to get him to outrank the maintenance man.

As the spring went by and the dust settled, I was getting ready for yet another year behind the iron curtain. I had taught summer school before and decided to do it again. At the time it was just to earn a little bit of extra money, but it ended up being necessary because of the mail I received a couple of months after the hospital episode.

In yet another act of insult and illegality, the school division's workers' compensation insurance denied my claim. The information provided to them by Butch and his office indicated that my episode was due to an underlying problem instead of workplace hazard. Rather than take responsibility for their reckless and wanton disregard for my health, Butch and company decided to shirk their ethical and financial responsibilities. Despite some heated phone calls with both parties, I was out of luck. Since I was still a member of the Democrat teachers labor union I figured it wouldn't hurt to ask for their help. Boy, I was wrong.

The same hack that had botched my first inquiry for help didn't fail to disappoint. She and the union's attorneys chose not to get involved and instead tie the matter in months of red tape. They cited "conflicts of interest" because representing me against the school system meant also representing me against other NEA members. Influential members of the organization feared the political complications that would come from fighting for one of its own members. Having already been apprised of the situation and having chosen to take no mitigating action, and after admitting responsibility in the hospital, both Colonel Custer and Butch were prime targets for civil suits as was the school division. Remember though, I'm a teacher and we can't cough up $400, let alone $400/hour for an attorney capable of recovering damages. With not much else left to do, I used the summer school income to pay the hospital bills and the thousand dollar five mile ambulance ride.

Not to be snookered again, I decided to be proactive about my schedule for the following year. I scheduled meetings with Colonel Custer, the scheduling educrat, and Mike. Despite what had happened only months ago and written warnings from my medical doctors and I, the educrats were long on promises and short on delivery. I was informed before graduation that my schedule would continue to include a late afternoon class, consequences to my health be damned.

By this point I knew the writing was on the wall, and I was actively being pushed to leave by my own accord. After record high AP test scores, a nomination for teacher of the year, and outstanding performance reviews, I was being guided toward the exit. This was when my previously passive and patient attitude changed forever. I knew that I had to become my own personal advocate because no one else would or could do it. Truthfully, I knew this all along but didn't want to admit that the system and union were as sickly corrupt as I knew they were.

The next year proved to be the toughest and also the most enlightening. I had no idea I was about to experience the real political power and depravity of government and its ability to destroy with impunity. The unadulterated and unhinged face of the Edutocracy was about to show its face.

Chapter Fifteen—Political Bedfellows

My academic pedigree and political experiences really shaped who I am. In the process of that shaping I learned a lot about naivety, calculation, and (sadly) deception. At the same time I learned the true value of honesty, deliberation, and reason. Out of the two came an attitude absolutely focused on making a change for myself instead of continuing to be a victim. Victimhood is like a cancer that is self-propagated, and I was sick of it.

Step one was completed when I got out of the Democrat teachers union. In order to do so, I had to make three phone calls, send a certified letter, and even threaten to call the Department of Labor to report pay fraud when dues were being withheld from my check. If you've ever wondered why Detroit, Chicago, and New York City are all bankrupt then look no further than these political action committees masked as protective labor unions.

I found myself enjoying the summer I had spent mostly paying the school division's medical bill by teaching summer school to functionally illiterate kids that had just failed my class during the school year. I was fortunate enough to connect over a cup of coffee with one of my teacher peers whom I really respected. He and I couldn't have had any less in common when it came to politics, but in terms of teaching philosophy and education reform we were almost in lock step.

The reason this kind of alliance is so important is because it exists so often and is not often recognized. Conservatives, Liberals, and Libertarians actually share a list of identical beliefs about education reform. Even though two of the three believe there shouldn't even be a Federal Department of Education because it is unconstitutional, they all agree that the system as it is today is broken. They also agree that student performance is the primary responsibility of the student and his parents and not teachers. We all agree, generally, that assistant principals, principals, and office educrats should not make salaries two to three times the salary of classroom teachers.

The particulars on how to get to these objectives differ, sometimes wildly. However, please name for me another issue where so many political adversaries have so much in common. Were these groups of teachers, not educrats, to unite around one central platform there would be no force powerful enough to defeat their ideas. This political panacea leaves educrats in mortal fear because it would spell the end of administratively-driven education and bring about the direct involvement of parents and taxpayers.

I wanted to find a way to show my peers they could find liability protection, avoid costly dues that go to political candidates, and be forced to support ideas that run counter to their educational philosophy. The answer to this dilemma was to ditch the NEA and NFT in favor of the local or state chapter of the American Association of Educators. In our case this organization is the Virginia Professional Educators. As a non-union organization, they offer teachers double the liability protection, a fraction of the dues, and the peace of mind to know their money will never be used for any political purpose.

One of our initial ideas was to borrow an idea from our peers in higher education via the creation of a faculty senate. After all, the instructional experts in the room are typically the teachers, not the administrators. We inherently know how best to teach our students while someone else counts the beans and makes sure the buses run on time. This body of teachers would have direct participation in the hiring of administration, instructional decisions, and school level issues. The locally elected school board would continue to hold political power to govern the district, but the intermediary money drain would be essentially eliminated, thus freeing up endless assets for instruction.

If you're familiar with Hugo's Les Misérables, or even America's founding days, then this next story will ring a bell. Before the revolution, nearly everyone knew the system was permanently broken, but few would dare say so. The private pounding of fists at the dinner table and the musings of small groups in private taverns were about as rebellious as things ever got. Eventually though, the system began to collapse and even the meek could no longer be silent. There is a point at which it is incumbent upon people who are stranded on a sinking ship to make the jump overboard. It is terrifying, and there is no guarantee things will immediately improve, but the ship is sinking either way. No amount of bilge pumping is going to change the inevitable.

Chapter Sixteen—Pravda

Novelist Bruce Coville wrote that "Withholding information is the essence of tyranny. Control of the flow of information is the tool of the dictatorship." My third year teaching in a public high school was when I really started seeing the enormity of the iron curtain. Once Colonel Custer had mounted his seat of power, he made no bones over his intention to lock the communication lines of the school down and take total control.

One of his first fiats was to ban employees, other than himself, from sending email to the faculty or staff listservs. Any and all communication being sent to more than three recipients was to be sent directly to the Colonel's office for screening and possible distribution to the faculty. To prevent any type of group discussions, no mass replies or forum types of email were permitted. Meetings rooms were to be scheduled and approved via the Colonel's office or by his lieutenants. Faculty members were discouraged from using their personal cell phones during the day like every normal professional does, and this decree was sent via the Blackberry Custer carried on his hip at all times.

Overhead announcements and pages were practically banned except those he made personally. The morning announcements and pledge of allegiance were no longer safe for students to read in the morning, so the Colonel had his own television station installed in the school. Each morning, teachers were to tune their televisions to this station so that we could watch his backside and listen to the Colonel recite the pledge of allegiance, grammatical mistakes and all. He dutifully read his pre-approved list of announcements and made a point to give commands over the air to teachers. Once in a while, the Colonel would allow students from a sports team to gather on screen and smile as they handed the previous night's sports trophy to him as if he was their father accepting their gifts. This kind of hyper egocentrism is the making of a special person.

In one particular set of cases, the coldness of the educrats hit a new low. A teacher friend of mine named Susan had recently discovered she was pregnant. She also had a pretty serious neurological disorder that required consistent medicine. Unfortunately, the medicine she needed was not safe to take during pregnancy. Protecting the baby by avoiding the meds resulted in serious seizures. Being the great mom and outstanding teacher she was, Susan tried to tough it out, and that she did for a long time. When she finally went on leave, the real trouble began.

Imagine you're on leave with two kids at home. You receive a call from your employer demanding that you return early from leave or face a non-renewal of your contract. Your peers are banned from donating leave, and you need to keep your job so you agree to return. You do so against the constant advice of your doctor and at the imminent risk to your long term health. Ultimately you have to decline to return the next year because you've been treated like garbage and have essentially been railroaded out of your job. All of this happens in secret.

Another colleague named Jill has a more serious issue, but it dealt with her newborn. Right after the baby was born it was evident that she needed open heart surgery. She had a serious and potentially fatal heart defect that could not be operated on until she was at least 12 weeks old. The snag came when Butch and Colonel Custer informed Jill that she may not be allowed to take the 12 weeks to see her newborn through open heart surgery. During a faculty meeting, one of Jill's friends tried to raise the issue and ask why teachers had been denied the ability to donate leave to Jill for her baby. Custer quickly silenced her with a glad hand and a verbose remark no one could understand. That candle was snuffed.

Finally, there was Kyle. One of the worst lapses of professional decorum and serious abuses of power I ever saw happened to Kyle. By the time you have read this portion of the chapter, I will have re-written it at least three times so as to edit out obscenities. It is common knowledge that educators and educrats are predominately progressive in their political ideology. Progressives readily admit that dominance over the field with few objections. Although their presence is much more obvious via higher education and radical Saul Alinsky acolytes, the power of the progressive movement in k-12 public education is just short of impermeable.

After my experience with the book burner my first year of teaching and my continued disgust at how professional teachers were being treated by educrats, I thought I was beyond surprise. When I met Kyle I was a little taken aback. He was an exuberant and kind guy that almost bowled you over with his positive attitude. In addition to be a Christian man and a good teacher, Kyle was also an active member of the Armed Services who had been deployed on more than occasion. The kids thoroughly enjoyed his class, and they learned consistently well.

The thing is, Kyle was openly and proudly a Conservative, America-centric man. He was also a scientist who recognized the reality of biology and biochemistry to the point where he welcomed kids of all races and sexuality into his classroom with blinders to difference. Much like me, Kyle routinely included lessons of character and good decision making in his classroom and through his demeanor. He had been teaching much longer than I, and he'd earned his post. Kyle's periodical deployments and non-compliant demeanor already infuriated Ethel and her comrades to the point where they openly mistreated and mocked Kyle whenever the opportunity arose.

Once Colonel Custer had established himself in the saddle, he quickly got to know Kyle and his reluctance to be a whipping boy for zealous educrats. Kyle was a marked man almost before school even began, and he (like me) knew it. By order of the Colonel, Ethel began a precision attack against Kyle's job. She harassed him for written lesson plans that she insisted on approving before he could teach. She sat in his class in order to ensure he was towing Custer's line and embarrassed him in front of students when he didn't. Meeting after meeting and one criticism after another, Kyle slowly wore down.

Ethel brought the weight of the edutocracy to bear on Kyle. She manufactured complaints, initiated grueling bureaucratic processes, and made his teaching day miserable. At one point Kyle and I began referring to the administrative office as the Central Planning Authority and hailing the hammer and sickle whenever she was in earshot. Beyond the jokes though, Kyle was being silenced like a fledgling newspaper critical of the state. When the time came to either renew contracts or decline to return, we lost Kyle. He'd been relegated to isolation in his classroom to the point where only one or two people really knew what had happened to him. This guy, who could check every box on the role model sheet, was the latest to meet the hammer of the edutocracy.

The control of people is only possible if you can control information. Keeping people ignorant is a part of keeping people compliant. To that end, it is vital to deny any dissenting opinion a public stage. If people are privy to how the sausage is being made then they'll quickly lose their taste for it. Instead, the herd has to be fed a vetted and preapproved set of information to keep them from panicking or becoming informed enough to upset the apple cart. If this sounds like something from Orwell's Animal Farm and you think it is a fantastic exaggeration, all I can tell you is what happened. The implications are yours to draw. Between Jane, Susan, Jill, Kyle and the unheard of other stories, one wonders exactly how such a travesty can continue on.

The truth is that my school district was only one among thousands of others across the country that are reliant upon suppression and sometimes outright criminal activity to stay in operation. A local government that has unchecked power being wielded by unelected educrats in the dark of night is a recipe for abuse. All the while real people are being aggrieved in total silence.

Chapter Seventeen—Hat Trick

You've met all of my antagonists like Custer, Butch, Ethel, etc. The folks I haven't talked enough about are the kids. As I oftentimes do, I use the words "kid" and "child" with caution because by the age of 17 and 18, many of these students are more mature than the average older adult. From working part time jobs that supplement their family's income to babysitting neglected younger siblings while their parents work hours from home or party like teenagers, it is amazing what these students do outside of school that would make us all proud.

The first mini story in this chapter has to be about Timmy. When I first heard about Timmy as a rising senior I was intrigued. I only knew him as the somewhat strange kid who was in the hallway lounges studying around 6AM when I arrived at school every morning. Mornings are my best time of the day, so coming in couple of hours early is well worth the lost sleep. Timmy would be there studiously buried in an AP exam review book. He was always polite and at least somewhat coherent at that hour of the morning.

Timmy came into my class as a senior with the kind of reputation that can make or break a kid his age. Not only was he already a college sophomore due to the number of credits he had earned through nearly perfect AP exam scores, but he also served as the school's counterbalance to dismal standardized test scores by scoring near perfect on them every year. At 17 he was nearly as well read as I was after I finished my undergraduate work. More importantly than all of that though, the young man was a teacher's dream.

As an Eagle Scout and practicing Mormon from a military family, Timmy was always that kid that was put up on a pedestal, sometimes to his own discomfort. Most striking was his humility about his success. What I first mistook for naivety was actually a full awareness of his gifts and a lack of hubris about any of them. Timmy routinely raised the standard for his peers to the point where his graduating class had some of the brightest minds I had ever encountered. There was fierce academic competition going on that really re-inspired me. What I went on to learn about Timmy throughout the year only served to cement what I saw in the classroom.

He was unceasingly loyal to his family and their blended ethnic cultures while at the same time balancing an extreme dose of self-placed stress to perform near perfection on everything he did. The few times I saw cracks in the armor I didn't know how he held it together, but he did. On his own initiative, Timmy was admitted to an Ivy League university as well as several other top tier colleges around the country. On top of that he was the division's first and only AP Scholar. Despite his accomplishments, and in spite of having done so in a public school, Timmy never received the recognition all of his teachers expected.

Mediocrity is like a pernicious virus. It duplicates and spreads to everything upon which it can cling until nothing exceptional remains. At his class's commencement, Timmy became the embodiment of a failed ideology's effect on an otherwise exceptional student. While some of his fellow graduates who could scarcely read were being cheered and lauded, Timmy and his other exceptional peers blended in like wallflowers. Never once was he recognized for outstanding achievement, invited to speak, or even named for a round of applause. After all, the egalitarianism of Custer, Ethel, and their ilk had to protect lower achievers from the possible embarrassment of being made to feel less stellar than Timmy.

At a moment when his family was packing its last cardboard box to move thousands of miles away and when he was at an impasse over how to fund his college career, Timmy kept his dignity. He could have been held up as a shining example and inspiration to his peers, but he was intentionally held down by Custer's boot. This young man had worked so hard and achieved so much that it stands to reason the educrats and system would have rewarded him thusly. Unfortunately, that didn't happen, but Timmy took it in stride and demonstrated poise at a time when I likely would have lost it on the nearest human being.

The educational system had never really handed him anything, and he never expressed entitlement. Partly because his parents instilled him with wonderful values, and partly because he was not used to asking for help, Timmy was smacked in the face pretty hard right when it seemed the worst was behind him. Because his family was neither destitute nor wealthy, he faced the same circumstance many young people do when they don't qualify for financial aid. The same educrats who had used him to prop up their broken system now denied him the means to continue his education. At one point, my family and another even considered cosigning his loan paperwork to get him there, but we were teachers, not principals.

As happy endings go, Timmy went on to attend an outstanding school that had been his second choice. He continues to flourish and amaze me whenever I have the chance to catch up with him. At a time when only about half of the young people who are in college actually have any business being there, Timmy is the exact type of mind that our society needs to be sending to higher education. People like him are our best hope at the next medical, engineering, and technological breakthroughs. I came away with two important lessons. First, Timmy isn't the first or last student to be let down by public schools. Lastly, when I volunteered to store his books for him after graduation I never imagined he was referring to rubber totes full of a virtual library of study manuals. I store them with pride.

****

If Timmy's story didn't make you feel inspired then this one surely will. Let me tell you about Karen. One of the disguised blessings (and sometimes thorn in the side) of teaching in public schools is that the students' ability levels vary wildly. Albeit uncommon, once in a while one of these seemingly low achievers blows the teacher away with gumption and perseverance.

Karen was pretty quiet in class. She obviously had friends and was pretty active in school activities, but she just wasn't much of a talker, at least to me. She struggled with my class from the first day because she was ill-prepared for the expectations to which I held my students. We don't do prefabricated worksheets and answer the textbook's chapter review questions. We engage with each other and actively learn.

Something about Karen's demeanor changed. She'd asked for my help when she wasn't performing well, and she took my advice to heart. She was already diligent about doing her work, but diligence does not a grade make. What she lacked in content knowledge and past study skills she more than made up for with a refusal to quit or accept an average grade. She pushed herself to her inherent potential, but I didn't know why until much later.

She told me once that she hated school because it was mechanical, and as she said, "boring." As far back as she could remember school was nothing more than repetitious busy work designed to fill time. She disengaged because the system disengaged her. Karen had the spark to be something great, but she was one of millions of children who unwittingly fall prey to the unspoken philosophy of public education in the United States—"Stuff 'em deep, and teach 'em cheap."

The semester wrapped up and Karen had really turned her performance around. More importantly, she did so because she earned it and not because it was given to her. At the organizational meeting for graduation I caught up with Karen and made some polite conversation about her plans for college or a career. As if she had been planning to tell me for a while, Karen said that she'd only recently decided to enroll in college to become a Social Studies teacher. Along with a memorable photo she sent me later of she and I in cap and gown, the best gift Karen gave me was a reminder that what I was doing wasn't always as pointless as it sometimes felt.

****

The last of what could have been dozens of student stories is about Bill. This story is a bit different than the rest because Bill wasn't a neat little bow-tied story about going to college. In fact, I don't think Bill will go to college. Since most of the students who go to college today have no business going there in the first place, I don't count this against Bill.

Bill was the definition of a homebody. He had spent his whole life in town and pretty much knew everybody. To the average observer there was nothing notable that would stick out about him, at least not as a student. Bill was a very talented athlete, and he was the kind of high school track and field athlete that could have gone on to professional competition had he wanted. He was admired by his peers and coaches because of his prowess and commitment to sports.

Although I have no interest at all in sports, I do have an interest in my students succeeding. Whenever I could, I committed to attending at least one of the kids' sporting events throughout the semester. I held my nose and went to one of nearly every sporting event each year for no other reason than to cheer on the kids. Oftentimes I went dressed in street clothes, a baseball cap, and sometimes a wig or something funny so that no one would recognize me. Teachers everywhere understand that situation.

The thing Bill had working against him was a wildly out of control temper. The guy was like the jolly green giant anyway, but when you added in his upper body strength he could have duked it out with the best of them. Although never once did I see him act violently, Bill was well known for his explosive temper. He yelled, he dented lockers, etc. One day his temper really flew off the handle.

I was on my way to grab a Coke and get ready for class when I turned a corner and saw Bill kick a recycling can about 25 feet down the hallway. His face was a read as a beet and I could see he was having an episode—likely over his on-again, off-again girlfriend. Just as one of the infamously authoritarian teachers was about to light into Bill, I waved her off and grabbed him by the arm. Yes, that is right my administrator friends; I grabbed him by the arm. Call child services.

I walked him to the student lounge and made him chill out. He was fuming and a hot mess. We talked for a few minutes and I finally got his hands to stop shaking long enough to see that he was not just calming down, but he was beginning to cry. I knew from his friends that Bill was actually a teddy bear in a pro athlete's body, but it still caught me by surprise to see tears in his eyes.

I leveled with him. "What the hell is wrong with you, bill? If that teacher had gotten to you first she would have had you suspended in a heartbeat." He gave me the classic grumbled and muddled evasive response. I knew him well enough as a student and a young man I liked that I could connect with him just a little bit. After asking him about his temper, Bill finally opened up a little bit. The rest of that conversation was well worth the time.

Without saying too much, I can tell you Bill came from a stressed home life. He and his siblings had been abandoned by one of their parents only recently, and he was working a part time job to help the household while also playing sports and trying to be a good student. The last thing on his mind was taking a deep breath and examining what his legendary temper was doing to his life. On top of it all, Bill was really bright. I pleaded with him for months to go to college because I knew his proficiency. Unfortunately, he didn't have the time to let his academic engine run full boar. At the moment he was facing some tough decisions about how to survive three more months of school and graduate without kicking trash cans down the halls.

Bill acknowledged how much of a problem his self-control had become. I gave him a safe zone to come to when he felt himself about to make a bad choice, and he even used it once or twice. More than that though, I got Bill to admit he was acting like a child instead of a young man. That got to him in a big way. Though I have seen him lose his temper a couple of times, even once at me, I can report happily that Bill has the self-control of a man now. He graduated with good grades, and he continues to mature (and stumble) as an above average member of society. Today, he is a friend of mine and I couldn't be happier about that.

The gifts teaching brings to teachers are too numerous to count. We are fortunate to do a job that has a lasting impact on people throughout the rest of their lives. Few of us will ever really be content because for every child we were able to reach it seems there is another one that we couldn't. Whether the failure to help a child succeed is the fault of the teacher or the system (or maybe both), we still take those positive and negative experiences to heart.

Chapter Eighteen—Matter of Life or Death

There are times when the decisions being made by Educrats don't just affect peoples' jobs or their reputations. In an environment that holds political correctness and diversity education as its penultimate credo, second only to obedience, the consequences for violating either are severe. This short chapter is a short example of what happens when it's time for the Educrats to walk their own walk.

I met a young man name Jeff. Having made his way into my class as a friend of my students, Jeff was excited to eat lunch with his upperclassmen friends. Although I didn't have Jeff as a student I quickly came to appreciate his sense of humor as well his manners. Like many of my other lunchtime companions, Jeff was heavily involved in the fine arts; he was a great drama student. After having met him and being around him in my classroom, I noticed that he was probably gay. Since he was one of many, I couldn't have cared less.

During one of our lunches, I overheard Jeff talking to his friends about the experience he was having in gym class and in the hallways. He was an effeminate guy, and he was being bullied pretty badly for that reason. Shortly thereafter, one of his friends asked to speak with me about Jeff. Being the brave and kind young man he was, this student shared Jeff's story with me and asked what he and I could do to stop the hazing being done to Jeff.

There are very few things that make me angry, but one of my short fuses is legitimate bullying. Now I'm not talking about the nanny state public relations campaign that calls normal teenagers bullies for calling his classmate "butthead." Legitimate bullying can be dangerous and ought to be taken serious-ly by all of us. With fuse lit and burning quickly, I marched to the chief of social justice's office.

The head guidance counselor, turned class scheduler, took the matter seriously ... or so I thought. She told me how much she empathized and assured me that action would be taken imme-diately to protect Jeff and punish the students responsible for pulling off his clothes and calling him "faggot" in the locker rooms. I left her office thinking that the matter was now in the hands of the administration and I could rest easy. After all, teachers are always told to take these types of issues straight to "the professionals."

I didn't hear anything about Jeff's situation for a while. How-ever, months after I left the school I learned that things hadn't gotten better. In fact, the administrators had done nothing more than pat Jeff on the head and give a half-hearted verbal correction to a couple of the bullies. Since my absence, Jeff had done the exact thing that I was trying to prevent. He attempted suicide.

His serious and nearly successful attempt at suicide was pro-voked by increasingly harsh hazing and bullying while at school. His friends had begged administrators for help, and several other teachers were aware of the situation. Despite edu-crats' tough talk protecting minorities, they couldn't be bothered with Jeff because, remember, I taught in the heart of the part of the U.S. where Jeff had "chosen" his biological and chemical makeup to become a homosexual and was going straight to Hell.

I nearly cried when I heard this story because I was unaware until months after it happened, and I was totally powerless to protect this young man. This same type of double talk and lack of follow-through is happening in your local school district too. Are you going to wait until your local Jeff actually succeeds at taking his life?

Chapter Nineteen—The Big College Lie

How many times have you heard the myth that college graduates earn, on average, a million dollars more over their lifetime than do non-college graduates? On top of being total bologna, this massaged statistic is dangerous. The college dropout rate is at a historic high, and that is a good thing. Let me tell you why.

Going to college is about pursuing knowledge and expertise. It never was and never should be considered a resume enhancer. Enrolling in college because it boosts the chances of getting a better job afterward is as dumb as it is pointless. In fact, we can all name at least a few people we know who make far more money than we do, and they never even thought about going to college. My garbage collector, plumber, carpenter, HVAC guy, etc., all make more money than I do with three degrees. This is a good thing! We need these jobs to be filled by young people who are able and willing to sweat for a living. The false entitlement to a desk job is as dangerous a plague on schools as anything else.

Thinking, let alone speaking, these words are an act of heresy in the public schools. Ask the scheduling department (formerly known as guidance counselors) about the subject. Both they and the Ethels of the world will tell every child they are entitled to a college education as a birth right. They will tell every junior to take the SAT and visit colleges, and they'll pressure every senior to report which institution they have chosen to attend for the purposes of putting it in the commencement program to inflate the division's profile.

The truth is that only about half of the students who go to college today have any business being there. A person's naturally inherited intellectual aptitude as well as their level of preparedness should determine their college plans. Many young people are kind and talented people with a lot to offer the world, but they don't have the academic prowess to pursue higher education.

Do you remember vocational schools? We used to teach young people that working in a trade was a strong and honorable career path. Students would take entry level jobs and work their way to the place they wanted to be over time. In the meantime, the students who were academically-oriented were encouraged to pursue higher education. The ones who chose neither path are more than fulfilling their level of ambition by doing those "other" jobs that entitled Liberal Americans disdain such as harvesting agriculture products and asking whether you want fries with your hamburger.

Not to be outdone by reality or reason, the egalitarians are insistent that teachers, parents, and support staff tell every child that they need to pursue higher education. The results of that hogwash are negative for all of us. Along with mortgage-sized debts that are insured by taxpayers, only a fraction of the students who enroll actually graduate. Now, they have to work at convenience stores and collect public assistance to survive, all the while blaming the college for their failure. Had we been honest with these students in high school or better prepared the marginally-ready students, these sad circumstances would be much less prevalent. However, in their minds they were denied the entitlement their high school promised.

Indirectly, the damage done to the academy is of serious concern. With more students being told they are entitled to go to college by birthright and regardless of whether they are literate, colleges and universities are stuck in a precarious position. They can keep their enrollment tightly restricted to control for quality as long as they are willing to accept minimal growth and the scorn of the political left. The other choice is to lower their standards to admit marginal students with the hope they can play catch up once they arrive. Along with bad students comes bad instruction.

As the lower achieving students are admitted and matriculate into classes, the faculty is met with embarrassment when they discover the students are at the academic level of an early high school student. They can't write in complete sentences, decode compound sentences, answer anything but multiple choice questions, or think critically. The first exam comes in with a high failure rate, and the students are all convinced it is the professor's fault for being too tough. Their own lack of preparedness never even crosses their minds because they were trained to avoid accountability at every turn.

Before you know it, the faculty encounters political pressure from bleeding heart peers and administrators which causes many of the faculty members to incrementally lower their expectations. The retention and graduation rates are dipping, and the donors and politicians want it corrected forthwith. The institution can continue to raise their tuition and fees indiscriminately because the Federal government will raise the borrowing limits on students to compensate. Meanwhile, the college or university becomes an enrollment factory focused almost exclusively on growing, paying exorbitant salaries, hiring three people for one job, and becoming a microcosm of the Federal government.

The last and most disconcerting consequence took a while to happen. As the years of college bloat went on through the 1990s and 2000s, a record number of young people earned bachelor's degrees. Now, these young people are out on the job market wondering why their degree didn't land them the overpaying desk job they were promised years ago. The value and respect that comes with degreed members of society has dropped precipitously. Having already degraded the value of a high school diploma to the point where it is a joke, the value of a bachelor's degree is already near the same point. That kind of intellectual decay can be cataclysmic for an advanced society that is depending on new medical technology, leaps in science, and more conscientious social scientists. Moreover, we are well into the process of taking these same intellectually-deficient graduates and recycling them into our college faculties, political positions, and public education so that the process can continue.

Chapter Twenty—Daddy Issues

One of the most common answers you'll get from a teacher about what is lacking in their students' lives is a father. Although I am proudly contemporary in my view that a two parent household, heterosexual or not, is best for a child, I think I understand teachers' responses. Don't get me wrong, I think one of the reasons our country is in the social doldrums it is today is a result of the government's bastardization of families, particularly Black families. Let's take liberty for the sake of argument and replace "father" with father figure or role model. The kids don't have many.

Aside from cultural pillars of character like Tim Tebow, Marcus Luttrell, and Robert Griffin III, there aren't the same types of great influences at home. They're surrounded by one or multiple combinations of unhealthy influences on a daily basis. Long gone are the days when you dreaded the words "You just wait until your father comes home."

Without understating the vital role that a mother plays in their child's life, especially when she has to because of an absent father, a man's role is profoundly different. Men instill a sense of strength and stability in children's lives that doesn't necessarily come from maternal connections. Dad used to be a super hero and a reasonable disciplinarian at the same time. Men, historically, have been the ones to teach their children about hard work and dignity. Once those role models are gone, so are the lessons.

Kids go to school today to find their role models. Not that there aren't some outstanding teachers and coaches still in public education, but the environment is much different now. The kids are taught that everyone gets a trophy at the end of the game because we don't keep score of winners and losers. We teach kids that on the first day of school they are to put their shiny new school supplies (that belong solely to them because the parents paid for them) in the middle of the room so that everyone in class can share so as not to embarrass the child of an illegal immigrant parent or irresponsible parent that bought none.

Coaches and teachers can barely shake a child's hand without being publicly castigated, or even worse, fired. Boys can't throw a couple of punches and settle a schoolyard argument because they are suspended for bullying. The notion that a child would receive a graded assignment back with red ink on it is so horrifying that teachers across the country are being banned from using red pens to grade. The gender bending that allows boys and girls to use each other's restrooms totally skews the kids' understanding of biological reality.

The role model is the school (the state). The school will provide free food and free services. Before and after school child care will be provided by the school. The school will protect the child from being innocently taunted by another seven year old after a kickball game. The school will decide what they are to learn and how they are to learn it. The maker of all decisions in their lives is the educrat.

I often made a sincere plea to my colleagues both in the preparation program and at school. Give a kid someone to admire. Suggest they join the Boy or Girl Scouts or the Boys and Girls Club. When you see a chance to teach a child like Bill a life lesson, do it! Coach a team of some kind and then pour everything you have into being a moral role model for kids. And yes, when a kid is crying or openly having a meltdown, for God's sake hug the kid. Look in their eyes and encourage them. Do something to let them know you give a damn about them. That kind of culture would spread like wild fire if we let it.

Partly because of the sick actions of a very few, but highly publicized, monsters who invade the innocence of a child and partly because of the near fanatic liability paranoia of school divisions, the teacher has been transformed from role model to government apparatchik. Tutoring a couple of kids after school in math is questionable, and giving a neighborhood kid a ride home after notifying the principal is tantamount to child abduction. In essence, the types of practices that made public schools a healthy and positive growing environment for children have been all but banned.

If you know a student who needs a mentor, jump in. When there is a student who always misses the bus, help them home. Take the child without a father and teach him what it means to be a responsible man. Show the girls in your class that you treat women with a precious respect instead of like a sex object. Demand the boys do the same. Above all, refuse to shy away from being more than a teacher to the kids for fear of your job. If enough professional adults push back against this debasement of role models then the system will be forced to change.

Kids don't have any control over their parents' poor choices. In light of that, we have to help, at least partly, to fill in the gap before the educrats do.

Chapter Twenty One—Keeping Your Powder Dry

One of the toughest parts of the job is knowing when to just walk away. There are so many battles to be fought that not even a contrarian like me could tackle all of them without going mad. Some of the battles I never tried to fight were the ones that had profound lessons to teach.

Each year, schools nominate faculty members to be the "Teacher of the Year." Those nominees go on to the district level, the state level, and national level where the president typically presents the national winner to the public. The process is relatively loose and many of us couldn't have cared less about it. Like most people, I cast a vote for the person I thought was best. It was only a few days later when I learned something very troubling. Normally, the teachers choose their nominee to go on to the next level and that is that. However, the new process for our school had been altered by Colonel Custer.

A secret and hand-picked committee of faculty and staff was chosen by Custer to collect the ballots and choose a winner by group consensus. I only learned about the process after one of the members of the committee came to me to share her serious concern over what she observed. Their discussion was to be confidential and their decision was to be heralded as totally independent. After counting the ballots, and just in case there was a chance for teachers' wishes to be honored, Custer instructed the committee to disregard the two names at the top of the list.

Whether because I was being mocked or because I had actually changed some heart and minds I'll never know, but I was at the top of that list. The person in second was equally maligned by the Colonel and dispensed with swiftly. I was humbled and honestly proud that I had won such an overwhelming number of votes. The big reveal in the local newspaper was a little bit of a surprise when we all opened it up to see one of our peers listed as the winner from our school. Don't misunderstand, we all thought he was a good teacher and most everyone liked him personally, but it was as plain as the nose on his face that he had been hand-picked by Custer's committee because of his near absolute compliance with Custer's policies. The situation was made worse when we tried to congratulate him because he knew he hadn't actually won, and he answered with a standoff-ish and blushing grunt.

The corruption wasn't always this insidious though. Once Tom left a lot of things were foisted upon the faculty that had been a long time coming. You'll remember I mentioned early on that one of the things a school division can do to make up for teachers' radically low pay is to give them some professional flexibility. Things as seemingly innocent as going across the street on our lunch break to get a hamburger or using our lunch and planning time to go to the bank. Although the edu-crats and their underlings regularly leave their offices and go out to lunch and run errands, teachers couldn't be trusted to use their personal time to do such outlandish things. In short order, Custer's minions created a written log upon which teachers could document special administrative permission they'd been given to leave campus.

Sold to us under the guise of safety, the next measure made our collective blood boil. When we returned for the first year under the Custer regime we were promptly lined up like cattle and forced to attach RFID chips to our badges. These new mandatory tokens tracked our entrance and exit from the building to ensure no local French fry violation went unpunished. At the time there was widespread grumbling among the faculty, and seeing this Custer ensured everyone that the purpose of this new tracking technology was to help him ensure everyone was accounted for during an evacuation.

Since most of the teachers fell for his line right away, those of us remaining were troublemakers when we complained to the educrats and Democrat teachers union. During the first break of the morning, and only moments after being boldly lied to by Custer, we encountered the new lead secretary explaining to a couple of late-arrivers that the new RFID tags were intended to track teachers hours—no mention of safety at all. Whether there was a staff member, or even two, that made poor choices about being on time for work was irrelevant to the fact that were all now carrying around RFID tags to track us like cattle. With the lies exposed and the perpetrators left unpunished for abusing their flexibility, the matter dropped from discussion like it was already old hat.

Soon thereafter came a clamp down on being allowed to be ill. Rather than follow the laws as they're written and requiring limited documentation after a certain number of consecutive missed days, Butch and Custer decreed that all leave taken must be accompanied by written explanations. If the teacher or their child was ill, it was expected that there would be a detailed explanation of the illness at 4:30 in the morning when the notice was transmitted from the sick person's home. In addition to being an overt breach of privacy to ask why an employee wanted to take one of their earned days of leave, this policy was particularly difficult for teachers with kids of their own. Just to screw with him, one cranky old drunk colleague of mine actually wrote Custer a detailed description of his gastro-intestinal issues during the flu.

Routines like this were slid into our already overflowing plates on a regular basis. In a sense, you learn to smile and nod your head until you can figure out which new initiative will last more than a week and which one you can ignore for the waste of time it is. If we were able to spend more time planning and teaching instead of being bovine secretaries, the kids would learn a great deal more.

Chapter Twenty Two—The Beginning of the End

My last year teaching at the high school started much like the ones before. My classes were scheduled contrary to the way they were promised, a new onslaught of regulations was coming down the pike, and the building had lost a dozen more teachers under Custer's regime. As if the previous year's events had never happened, I jumped in with both feet yet again. I knew that retaining my position this third year would require some dramatic changes.

The rise of the blight that is the Common Core state standards hadn't been adopted in Virginia, at least not by that name. However, the bevy of new burdens on teachers and changes to curriculum were nothing more than an equal pox by another name. In addition to being morally broken, our faculty was being further pressured to "close the achievement gap." In educrat code this means the minority populations' test scores were too low and their dropout rate too high, so the teachers needed to find a way by hook or by crook to close the gap. In addition, the number of disciplinary actions involving minority students was far greater than that of white students, so each teacher was instructed to be culturally sensitive when dealing with discipline. As we said before, the gap is artificially closed when the high achievers are torn down.

Teachers were being forced to take on accountability for their students' choices. Instead of teaching children and then encouraging the child and his parents to make good choices, the teacher would now be evaluated over actions totally out of our control. Giving the child every resource they had to offer and teaching like an all-star was no longer going to placate the egalitarians. This highly subjective and educratic measure was go-going to be enforced, and seriously at that. Teachers would be held to account for whether a student studied for a test, couldn't read since kindergarten, or was just a naturally low performer. Although most of us were able to short circuit the nonsense by displaying growth from the beginning to the end of the time we spent with the student, there was still a lot of negative pressure placed on teachers for students' choices.

What only two years before had been a vibrant and positive learning environment had now been totally transformed into a miserable experience for everyone. Custer was riding high on accolades that conditions had improved in the eyes of the central educrats. What none of them could or would see is that the rate of teacher exodus under his regime was nearly as high as the record number he'd racked at his previous prison, and this year would be the worst yet. With not one notable measure of success, Custer had finagled himself into the role of the turnaround artist.

Teachers looked different. It was like there was a slow dirge playing all of the time, and all but the true believers could hear it. The kids acted more like robots than teenagers, and the academic picture didn't improve either. Student lounges where Tom had designed safe and viewable places for the kids to spend their few free minutes had all been closed and turned into makeshift storage and classrooms. Arriving students were held in a common room until moments before the day started so that there wouldn't be any socializing or morning interruptions to the Colonel's order. Students were ushered out of the hallways so fast after the bell that they couldn't even pack their bags before a minion would yell at them to vacate the building or be punished for trespassing. Scheduling before and after school study sessions was like asking for a millions dollars, and any chance to mentor a kid was gone completely.

The educrats at the central office rode the high too. Between late night private poker games filled with confidential gossip and alcohol to outright showboating about the heft of their accomplishments, the ruling class was ensconced, and they knew it. At one point, a former student of mine chanced upon Custer at a local big box store, and this former student told the guy exactly what he thought of him. Polite or not, this now taxpaying adult spoke his non-threatening piece to a public servant, which he was legally entitled to do. The response was pretty short and predictable. "You better learn to show me some respect, boy. I'm a respected member of this community, and everybody around here knows who I am. You don't know who you're talking to." For her part, the division superintendent, whom, I affectionately call Evita, continued her full throated support of the Custer regime.

At one point early in the year, I was privy to an unexpected and very sad comment by Mike. He'd been teaching for nearly 20 years and was known for his eternally positive attitude. The kids always saw the energy he brought into class, and it was infectious. However, even Mike had a breaking point. One day I decided to eat lunch with a couple of the older faculty members. I found myself relating much better to them than most of the younger folks. During the brief period we had to inhale our food, Mike stunned all three of us at the table.

I asked him about his day so far. With this pale and empty face Mike looked at me and said, "This is the first time during my career that I don't look forward to getting up to come and teach." Those words may not come across to the casual observer as powerful, but when he said it, the three of us just sat in silence. Coming from Mike, this was like hearing Santa say he was tired of Christmas. Between the constant barrage of micromanaged administrative garbage being piled on him by Colonel Custer, his responsibilities as a classroom teacher, and his duties as our department leader, he was just spent.

The unspoken truth was that everyone who was smiling was doing so either because they needed to fake it for the kids or because they'd been drafted into Custer's army. There is a point at which the fuzzy feelings about changing the world and touching children's lives simply don't offset the hidden abuse teachers suffer. This is the dangerous tipping point when teaching becomes a job in its traditional sense and ceases to be a passion and profession. That hurts the kids far more than it does the teachers.

Chapter Twenty Three—Full Disclosure

I've told you a lot of stories I've never shared before. In fact, I had to make some hard decisions about which things were still too sensitive to discuss. There are experiences I still have to safeguard due to safety and sensitivity issues. After all, teachers' first priority is to protect kids. Changing names, gender, and identifying characteristics is a fully professional way to go about writing a pseudo-memoir, but even those contrivances won't confuse the subject of the stories.

If you had to imagine what would be the worst circumstance for teachers to face in their profession, what would it be? In New York, Philadelphia, and other urban areas that are dominated by labor unions, there are hundreds of teachers that are paid full time salaries without ever being allowed into a classroom. This administrative duty is often the result of those stories you see on the evening news about some complaint by a student or parent. Aside from the waste of money and the unethical way that money is being squandered, administrative duty assignments are complicated.

People are relatively familiar with at least one story about a bad teacher or a sexual pervert that ends up in the headlines. That realm of discussion also has an inherent bias against the adult. Fortunately, parents and teachers are more aware now than they used to be about the deviant actions of a select few bad people. Along with that awareness also comes a tendency to slowly but surely creep into disproportionate liability avoidance. Avoiding an embarrassing story in the local paper or a national headline is a reasonable expectation for any school division, but when that kind of legitimate diligence becomes institutional ass covering, there is a real problem.

Statistics tell us that three out of every four allegations made against a teacher are proven to be baseless and consequently dismissed. I cannot stress this next point enough—once an allegation has been made against a teacher the damage done to their reputation is permanent. It wouldn't matter if the accuser recanted, they wrote an apology for the record, or the teacher was shown on video to be in the Bahamas on vacation during the alleged incident. The stigma that is attached to a teacher when she is accused of innocently brushing by a boy's face with her breasts is fast spreading and permanent. Credible or not, what you must understand is that the point is not the nature of the evidence or quality of the investigation, but instead the seriousness of the charge.

In one instance before my time at the high school, one of the teachers was accused of threatening a child with a knife. According to the children, the teacher was cutting some type of food with a large sharp knife ... like most adults do. She was accused of having threatened to injure the child with the knife. Common sense ought to have told everyone that the teacher, if she said anything at all, was making a completely innocent joke that no reasonable person would argue. Whether she actually made a threat or how she said what she did is irrelevant to the fact that she was accused. This teacher was suspended for a period of time before being allowed to return. No one quite knows what, if any, punishment she endured or whether the accusation was founded, but her reputation is now inextricably linked to that incident where she may or may not have actually done anything wrong.

The natural counter to this seemingly teacher-favoring argument is that a real accusation may fall through the cracks, thus resulting in harm to a child. On its face that argument is reasonable enough, but the details matter. Students and parents are not naïve. In the current "Me" generation, an overzealous parent, child, or group of people can move heaven and Earth if they level an accusation at a teacher. They can often pressure a weak-kneed administrator or school division into capitulating to their petty demands under threat of lawsuits or public attention. This list of reasons for making an accusation also leaves out the most insidious of the motivations—a coordinated plan to push a teacher out.

The investigation that is supposed to be done after an accusation is made is important for all parties. This supposedly impartial inquiry typically involves written statements from the accuser, any witnesses, and other supporting information. Interviews are held and all of the information is absolutely mandated to be shared with the accused with the exception of the accuser's name when there is a safety concern. Along the way, the stories of the accuser and other parties are to be compared for common information and inconsistencies. Moreover, any child or teacher wishing to offer information germane to the inquiry is legally entitled to do so. The responsibility of the inquirer is to gather as much pertinent information as possible in order to allow for a just adjudication of the matter. Sadly, this level of professional courtesy and ethical standard of decency is often violated. In all cases, the confidentiality of the teacher's employee file is legally sealed except by court order or consent of the teacher. Unauthorized disclosure of confidential information regarding an inquiry, especially when that disclosure is intended to inflict harm, is a serious crime.

Without an impartial internal affairs department or independent oversight mechanism, the only barrier between an educrat and a crime is the skill of the criminal. Against an often powerless subject like a teacher, a self-contained school division has both the theoretical and practical means to do unspeakable damage to a person without any repercussions. Much like an attorney general vowing to investigate himself, the notion is ridiculous to the point of insanity.

With nothing more than a selectively interested Democrat teachers union and a self-contained school division that has the powers of judge and jury, there is nothing to stop a teacher from being abused by the system. We remember Butch telling us that teachers can't afford attorneys or the time off from work, so we often get so daunted with the accusation that we feel hopeless. This potential for injustice is one of the biggest reasons why teachers seek liability protection from an organized group such as a union or professional organization. The minimal investment in that membership may end up being worth a great deal.

Chapter Twenty Four — Custer's Last Stand

The last thing a normal new teacher would worry about is the possibility that they may be on the receiving end of some surreptitious ousting by their school division. We're focused on teaching and surviving in a broken system. At the time, I was well aware of the serpent like nature of the educrats and their comrades, but I never expected what was coming my way.

The first time I tried to write this chapter of the book, I could feel my blood pressure rising in my flushed face just from the thought of telling the story. After a severe psychological trauma, our natural response is to bury it and move on. In some cases I understand that reaction. The last thing someone wants to do is relive an unpleasant experience. However, in cases where that event has long-term implications for one's everyday life there is little utility in simply wishing it away. I've tried both, and you can see clearly here that I've given up on giving up.

I made a couple of bad decisions when I was teaching. I disciplined a guy for wearing a hat in the building when it was actually a different guy. We resolved that one. I called Ethel a "bitch" after she accused me of being a racist, which I regret only because it was pointless. I also allowed a girl to pass my class by violating my own class rule and giving her extra credit due to prolonged supposed depression and her helicopter father. Although I am sure there are probably a couple more, I can say confidently I never made a decision that violated either mine or my employer's implicit ethical standards, let alone rules. All of my remaining faith in the system was erased when I came to school on a seemingly regular Monday morning.

As I walked into the building I noticed Butch was there. On its own, this was uncommon for being so early in the day. When I came into the office suite, I was greeted by Custer and his Foghorn Leghorn "Mornin' Brine, come chat with me." I followed him down the hall to his cave and there sat Butch. Given my already tenuous rapport with the educrats, especially these two, I knew something unpleasant was coming.

As I sat there and listened to Butch deliver his fragmented sentences, I think time slowed down. I was hearing him, but I couldn't believe what he was saying. I was accused by a student of having made a perverted comment toward them. Upon hearing the student tell this story, another teacher had reported the incident to Ethel who then passed it on to the Colonel. Half waiting for one of them to lean over and spit into the trash can between sentences, I sat in disbelief.

After obviously dismissing the whole silly accusation, I expected to hear that I could go ahead and get ready for the day. Instead, like a suspect on a television drama purp-walk, Custer informed me that I was on paid leave until further notice while an investigation was conducted, and then he escorted me out of the building. Partly out of bitterness and also because it was painful, that was the last time I ever set foot on the property—I even stayed away from the kids' graduation.

After taking this punch out of nowhere, I was instructed by Butch to discuss the matter with anyone. Actually thinking he had the authority to make such a decree, I knew I had to get on the phone right away to straighten out the mess. I called the woman who, at the time, I actually looked at like a pseudo mom. Hope reminded me of my mother in the sense that she was an amazing listener, very honest, and trustworthy with no exception. Both were Christian women that had no hesitation telling me when I was acting like a horse's ass. Since I only lived a couple of miles away, I raced home to get on the phone.

I called Hope to tell her what had happened, and I can only imagine she was as shocked as me. She gave me some reassuring words and wished me luck and support. Even though he was no longer in the system, I even called Tom to ask for his counsel, which he gave gladly and so graciously. Having only been a member for a couple of months, I called the new group I had fought so hard to advertise, the Virginia Professional Educators. My next step had to be obtaining experienced representation.

Imagine being in such a daunting situation and having been ordered by Butch to do nothing. I was expected to sit around and wait while two men I wouldn't trust with a nickel were conducting an investigation into a load of hooey that could impact my career. Since I've never been the compliant type and given how badly I had been treated by these two in the past, I decided to play this round my way.

Knowing full and well who the student was that had made the ridiculous statement, I was immediately comforted by the fact that at least a dozen other students were already somehow informed of the situation and ready to set the record straight. This same student, the mother actually, had been upset with me for evaluating one of her child's recent essays poorly. Not to be outclassed by a little old teacher, this was their retribution for the grievous injustice the student felt had been suffered. It was only months later that I learned this same family had taken similar action against teachers in the past with success—so why not do it again?

Equipped with at least a dozen witnesses and their verified supporting stories, my representative and I were confident that I was going to be able to navigate this storm successfully. What neither of us accounted for was the counter party's wanton disregard for this impartial process. After calculatedly deciding not to take written statements from the accuser or his contrived co-conspirators, the entire cabal morphed into a fishing expedition. Every feeling I had ever hurt and every teenage grudge I had against me was compiled into a laughable "list" of a few instances of insensitivity.

I was still hopeful because I knew I had the truth on my side and ways to support it. As far as I knew, I was innocent of any wrongdoing absent verifiable evidence to the contrary. Again, I made an assumption based on decency and ethics, of which Butch, a former failed police officer, elementary school teacher, and principal had none. When students began lining up and making appointments to share their stories to dispel the accusation, they were turned away. They were told they no longer needed any information and had already made their decision. I found out much later that the accuser was called into the office and told point blank by Butch, "We already know what happened and we believe it, so we just need you to agree."

The text messages and well wishes poured in. Unbeknownst to me, a few hundred students drafted and circulated a petition that they thought would shed light on the situation. I had taught them about justice and republicanism, but those lessons didn't turn out to be effective in this case. I was relegated to sitting at home and waiting to hear about developments whenever and however I could get them. Custer was so resentful of the public outcry that he included my stirring of a "resistance" in his complaints against me. This was particularly laughable in light of the fact that I was entirely unaware of the whole movement.

My organization representative guided me through the meetings and developments with a sober and reliable firmness that is partly responsible for keeping my sane. To add insult to injury, one of the side effects of my neurological affliction is increasing severity of symptoms with the increasing level of stress on the body's neurological system. I was beginning to relapse at a time when I had only recently found a stable, albeit diminished, balance for my health.

Following unsuccessful attempts at rational conversations with Butch and pleas to Evita, it was increasingly clear that the educrats had made their decision. Students who had attempted to disclose the truth were still being rejected for appointments, their parents were being ignored, and the school board was willfully ignorant just the way the educrats intended them to be. Colonel Custer went so far as to start interrogating and threatening students who voiced opposition to the modern day witch hunt. During a student council meeting, one of my best former students was publicly excoriated by Custer for daring to challenge his abusive approach to the situation. I was particularly proud when she reminded Custer that she paid his salary—a favorite line of mine which happens not only to be demonstrably true but also poignant for a tax-paying young woman coming into adulthood.

After several difficult conversations and seeing the recalcitrant position of these corrupt school officials, I was nearing physical immobility due to the disease, and I had been out of school for a couple of weeks. By that point there were only two options available. The first was to fight the accusation by filing a formal appeal to which both parties agreed I was entitled. All of the evidence as well as the consistent discrediting of the accuser would have certainly resulted in my reinstatement, a fact to which Custer later secretly admitted. Option two was to resign my position due to the serious degradation of my health.

Fighting is what I've always done. I've never shied away from conflict because I would rather lose the administrative argument and retain the virtue of principle even if that was the best possible outcome. I've walked away from jobs and people over principled disagreements, all of which I would repeat 100 times over. There is something about a person with principle that is increasingly rare today. I was raised better than cowardice in the face of adversity.

Right when we were about to make the decision to fight through the mess and retain my position, we received a discouraging but predictable message from Butch. Even if I had succeeded in my appeal, Custer had made the administrative decision not to renew my contract for the following year, which happened to also be my tenure year. I had aggravated a maniacal control freak by defying him, and that kind of defiance is intolerable for an authoritarian. In spite of almost three school years of nearly perfect performance evaluations, outstanding student performance, and accolades from peers locally and regionally, I was being dropped like a bad habit. That kind of power has no check or protection, and it happens to great teachers every day.

With a heavy heart but a clear conscience I prepared my resignation letter and a goodbye email to the staff. After transmitting the farewell via email I drove the mile or so to the educrats' office to hand deliver my resignation to Butch. I felt a visceral need to hobble into the building and look the snake in its eyes. If I was going to go down then the very least I would accept was doing so with gritted teeth and boldness. Not to be confused with hubris or the perception that I felt some sense of self-flattery, I knew that I held both the legal and moral high ground.

At first glance it may not be clear why I decided to voluntarily walk away. The truth is that even if I had been willing to withstand the social stigma to which I would be exposed for another 5 months, there was no way my body would let me get that far. By the time I submitted my resignation, the level of meds I was on all but destroyed all of my hair follicles, leaving me nearly bald, and the toxicity was beginning to affect my liver. I was losing peripheral vision in one of my eyes because of the stimulants, and living in a three story home had become nearly impossible because I couldn't climb stairs. Although I was initially weary of including these details in the book, I think it's important for people to know that behind even the toughest personalities there are often complicating factors totally unknown to other people. When decisions like the ones Butch and Custer made come to fruition, real people are hurt, and it isn't a game of brinksmanship. No public employee, elected or otherwise, should have that amount of unchecked destructive power against his master.

Chapter Twenty Five—Sitting Bull Won

No sooner had I finished my brief exchange with Butch, I received a phone call from a family friend. I was driving through the fast food lane when she asked me what was going on. Thinking she was asking about the broader situation I told her I had resigned earlier in the morning. She interrupted and said, "Brian, I'm talking about the emails."

I was confused at first, but then she read them to me over the phone. Unbeknownst to me, someone had circulated a series of email conversations to nearly every teacher, assistant principal, principal, central office, and school board member. Since I had been locked out of my school email immediately following my resignation, I didn't receive the messages until this friend was kind enough to forward them to me. The content was both awful and vindicating at the same time.

In heavily redacted images, the rest of the picture become clearer to everyone involved. In the email, the sender explained that they saw the email conversation open in the teacher workspace on another teacher's computer. The person reported themselves to be a teacher and to have shared the conversations anonymously because they currently had a child in the school system and feared retribution. The same person claimed to have held onto the conversations hoping that the outcome would have been different, but my early morning resignation prompted the release. Transmitted between two private email accounts off of the school system's server, this exchange of filth really gave people an unvarnished look at the version of Colonel Custer I had been trying to communicate since his arrival.

The two people, one being Custer and the other being an unidentified seemingly male teacher, carried on a dozen or so messages about me and my situation. The two were golf buddies and had an ongoing rapport outside of school. During the conversation Custer openly admits "That's the thing, I don't think he [Brian] did any of it. It sounds like a mess of pissed off kids." After referring to me as a "closet queer" and a "trouble maker," Custer goes on to write "Yeah we'll just bluff him into thinking we have something so he'll quit. [Butch] wanted to fire his ass last fall when he pulled that disabilities act routine I told you about. We couldn't though because he'd had that dike from the VEA sue." These juvenile slurs and comments about me and the VEA representative were hard enough for me to read that I half hoped they weren't real.

I sat in the parking lot of a local store and just listened as people called me and texted me asking if I was alright. Truthfully, I didn't know what to say. One would think I would have felt vindicated, and I guess I did, but not yet. The emails had gone out to over a hundred people. In the release note, the sender had issued an ultimatum to the school division that promised to continue releasing incriminating documents if the situation wasn't resolved. These documents purportedly included additional conversations about the covered-up use of racial epithets by a teacher, Jane's situation with breast feeding, and other tasteless stories. By that time though, I was already gone. My resignation was official, and no amount of apology by Custer or Butch could have healed the damage that had been done.

It isn't that I didn't appreciate the sentiment behind what the sender was trying to do. I recognize that the person was trying to help in their own way, but the fallout from the distribution of that kind of unfiltered content is intense. Though he predictably denied the emails were real, I know in my gut they were. He writes the way he speaks, and for a well-read person that is easy to see. Notwithstanding what looks like the scrambling of dates on the emails, the whole thing wreaked of a true to life conspiracy. I'm actually happy the rest of the information was never sent out because I think enough harm had been done at that point, and the lipstick was off the pig.

As a matter of record I was able to retain good standing with all of my credentials and references and also be able to truthfully say I left of my own accord. Once the cons outweigh the pros of a situation, sometimes you have to just stop the bleeding. If you're going to lose a fight, you ought to lose with your dignity.

Months after the waters had calmed and I had forgiven the parties involved, I came home to two pages of information I certainly was not surprised to see. Someone who was still on team Brian read me into a social media conversation between the entitled brat who had made the accusation against me as well as his equally unindicted coconspirator. In this short exchange that took place during the height of the ordeal, both boys talk about their efforts to manufacture the story, falsify testimony, and mislead everyone involved. Even today I don't know who obtained the conversation, but I can surmise it was someone who was more interested in the truth than a childhood friendship. Frankly, the content is what I care most about, and even though I never followed up by sending this conversation to the school division, I am satisfied that it eventually made its way around the entire school population.

Chapter Twenty Six—Lessons Learned

I'm not even sure that this is the first appearance of lessons learned. Really, this whole book is about lessons I learned while I was behind the iron curtain. Since I escaped the edutocracy, my interest and informed opinion of public education have developed even more. While keeping in mind that my experience was not typical of all systems, I am still able to discern the aspects of my experience that are shared by thousands of other teachers around the country.

One of the wake-up calls I try to share with everyone is that they're just as susceptible as I was to the abuse of power by educrats. Following my departure, another teacher was embroiled in a similar but less publicly known ordeal from which he was able to recover, albeit with a forever marred reputation. At the end of that school year, several more faculty members either resigned or were not uninvited back. Whether because they wouldn't conform to Custer's regime or because they found greener pastures I don't know, but I am happy to see an exodus from that place. As one of my colleagues said to me before graduation, what happened to me "… scared the Hell …" out of people to the point where no one will say a word. I don't blame any of those folks for failing to come to my defense because they also had children and responsibilities that required them to retain their jobs. I do wonder, however, how the situation would have resolved if the faculty, in its collective voice, had simply refused to let one of their peers be abused by a power-drunk educrat. The same man who had been awarded a principal of the year award years earlier had been exposed.

The benefits of having taught high school are permanent. I periodically receive kind messages and phone calls from former students talking about their college careers and future ambitions. Seeing them succeed and hearing them say "Thank you" is really the icing on the cake. At one time I regretted the fact that I'd written letters of recommendation for some former students based on who I perceived them to be, specifically the accomplice involved in the false accusation. When posed with the decision about whether I should rescind or revise my recommendation, I did what I thought was best for both of us. I didn't say a word. Having called in a couple of favors to get the kid admitted into his preferred school without him even knowing it, I didn't see any benefit from derailing his future. I just tell myself that once he gets older and matures perhaps he will eventually start to understand the gravity of what he did.

I quickly returned to the education realm as instructional designer, college professor, and professional writer. Almost as if I had taken a useful detour, I'm infinitely more informed having experienced the life behind the iron curtain of public education. Admittedly, I have half-heartedly pursued some leads to return to other school divisions because I miss the interactions with curious minds and energetic kids. In a lot of ways, I fed off their energy and that motivated me to constantly improve. Nonetheless, I continue on with a honed focus on being a better teacher and better person regardless of what job I am doing.

Chapter Twenty Seven — Open Windows

Have you ever contemplated what you'd do if you suddenly came into a bunch of money? I think we have all pondered the things we could do with more resources, but again I am an odd duck. After I paid off a little debt and bought Sarah anything she wanted, I'd end up investing the rest in a school. One of the reasons I wrote this book is because our country is well beyond having a conversation about public education. We're all disenchanted with the broken system and looking for answers.

The government has a monopoly on education right now. Even though private schools are increasing in number and enrollment, the de facto education chosen by the vast majority is the public system. The only option for most non-working poor as well as working families is to just hope the public system is good enough. In the face of the radical educrats and politicians who fear vouchers and charter schools because of their siphoning of tax dollars out of the monopoly, taxpayers are increasingly cynical about how their money is being spent. They have this crazy notion that public education monies ought to be spent teaching kids to read, write, and do math instead of funding a failed and bloated education welfare program.

In my perfect school dream, parents would run the whole operation. A rotating board of parents would choose the school's leaders, the curriculum, and set the standards for enrollment. Potential teachers would be interviewed by parents and not just an administrator. We'd nurture the intellect of every child and also treat them like growing people instead of robots on an assembly line. Critical thinking and respectful disagreement would be treasured instead of penalized.

I am determined to make this dream happen. I have no idea how I am going to make it happen, but I think God gives us a means when there is a real need. If creating another income stream or soliciting donors is what it takes, then that's the work I'll do. I believe strongly that you have to have some skin in the game if you want people to take you seriously about a big endeavor like starting a new school. In that spirit, I fully intend to use as much of the proceeds as I possibly can from the sales of this book to serve as the seed money for a school where teachers can finally teach, kids can finally learn, and principles actually matter.